Love No Matter What

*When Your Kids Make Decisions
You Don't Agree With*

Brenda Garrison
With Insights from Her Daughter Katie

THOMAS NELSON
Since 1798

NASHVILLE   DALLAS   MEXICO CITY   RIO DE JANEIRO

Published in Nashville, Tennessee, by Thomas Nelson. Thomas Nelson is a registered trademark of Thomas Nelson, Inc.

Published in association with KLO Publishing Service, LLC (www.KLOPublishing.com).

Thomas Nelson, Inc., titles may be purchased in bulk for educational, business, fund-raising, or sales promotional use. For information, please e-mail SpecialMarkets@ThomasNelson.com.

Library of Congress Cataloging-in-Publication Data

ISBN 13: 9780849947414

Printed in the United States of America

13 14 15 16 17 QG 5 4 3 2 1

To my daughter Katie.
Thank you for your patience and
love as we journey together.

Contents

Acknowledgments

Thanks so much to Gene and our daughters—Katie, Kelsey, and Kerry—for their constant encouragement, support, and love.

Thank you to my agent, Kyle Olund, who encouraged me through this process. Kyle, thanks for patiently waiting for me to arrive at the right time to write this book.

Special thanks to the families and adult children who shared their stories. Without you this book would not be possible.

Introduction

I love seeing the results of my efforts. I love seeing an empty laundry room at the end of laundry day. I love seeing the numbers on the scale go down when I eat healthy and exercise. I love seeing the look on my family's faces when I place a beautiful meal on the dining room table. So as a parent, I thought if I kept doing all the right things I knew to do, I would see the results of my three daughters walking with the Lord and making (mostly) good decisions.

As a young mother I listened intently to Christian parenting experts' advice on how to handle everything in my kids' lives, from media and entertainment to friends and devotions. I thought I heard them promise that, if I did everything right, my kids would turn out right. My results-oriented thinking translated their teaching to "A + B = C." A and B represented good parenting advice and C represented a perfect kid. But one thing I do not remember hearing is that sometimes our best efforts do not produce our desired results. When it became evident to my husband, Gene, and me that our oldest daughter, Katie, was going to chose her own path—one that wasn't parallel to God's—we asked ourselves what we did wrong. Actually, I asked myself that. Gene, being much wiser, knew we had done our best.

Please know that our best was nowhere near perfect. For

Katie, being the oldest child of two inexperienced parents meant a lot of trial and error in parenting her. Katie was a fussy baby from about two weeks old. Even the oldest and most experienced moms we knew did not have a clue how to make her happy. As Katie grew, so did the frequency of her challenges to Gene and me. For Katie, being asked to do something wasn't enough motivation to do it. It had to matter to her personally, and even then she acted in her own time. She was strong-willed. Gene and I didn't know about this personality type, and we certainly did not know how to parent her accordingly. It was as if we and our child were speaking two different languages.

My "A + B = C" strategy was shot full of holes with each of Katie's decisions we didn't agree with. She did not care how we were trying to parent her. She wanted her way. Period.

The day Katie dropped a bombshell of a decision on us, she shot the fatal hole in my strategy, and it limply drifted to the floor. I realized then that the equation of our lives would never resemble "A + B = C" and that the only formula I needed for my parenting was one that showed my daughter *love no matter what*. I have learned much in the past seven years, and I'll do my best to share it with you.

Katie and I have learned to journey together. One of my greatest delights was Katie agreeing to add her perspectives to the book. She and I still don't agree on some issues of faith and politics, or her belief that we need for a sister-cat for our cat, but we have a healthy, honest relationship. We are each other's biggest cheerleader. I think you'll find encouragement in Katie's comments and insights as she gives you a peek inside your child's head and heart.

One parent's story that has been a constant source of help

and encouragement is that of the father of the prodigal son in the parable Jesus tells in Luke 15. I have learned much from the example of this father, who showed steady love without being too harsh or too lenient. I hope you will find his example helpful as I share it throughout the book.

The first five chapters of the book help parents see where they are and how they got there. The second half of the book helps parents build healthy relationships with their kids. In chapters 6 through 10, you will decide if you're willing to make changes in your relationship with your child. Unless you're willing to cooperate as God speaks to you to change you, none of the information in the book will be helpful. True life change comes only as we listen to and obey God. My words are only as valuable as the paper on which they are printed, so I urge you to read and study the referenced scriptures. Pray and see how God would speak to you and how He may be working in you. Then cooperate with Him. You can trust God for what's best for you and your child.

I know our story is not as desperate a situation as many families face, so I have talked with many parents and a few of their kids about their variety of experiences. I will share their stories and insights throughout the book. Below is an introduction to the families (in alphabetical order) with whom you will be journeying.

- Aaron, son of Julie and Marty—Aaron stopped going to college . . . without telling his parents.
- Allison, daughter of Donna and Bob—Allison was so strong-willed that she married a man her parents actively cautioned her against marrying.
- Andrea, daughter of Cynthia and Frank—When Andrea was in college, she announced to her family she was a

lesbian.

- Andrew—Angry, alone, and with no father figure in his life, Andrew made choices that led to his living in a state-run facility for troubled youth.
- Brennan, son of Deb—Brennan's poor choices led to drug use, DUIs, and two prison terms.
- David, son of Jan and George—David has struggled with depression and the use of alcohol and drugs.
- Grace—Grace was in college when she began her journey to discover who she was. Her parents disagreed with her choice of boyfriend and her decision to live with him.
- Greg, son of Lisa and James—Greg has self-esteem issues that led to substance abuse and a disrespectful attitude, especially toward his father.
- Isaac—Isaac used and sold drugs.
- Jeremy, son of Connie and Robert—Jeremy smoked marijuana with his friends and saw no problem with it.
- Keith—Keith's parents didn't agree with his decision about his college major.
- Nathan, son of Susan and Gary—Nathan started drinking alcohol in junior high, and his abuse of alcohol spiraled downward in high school and in his young adult life.

No matter the gravity of our kids' decisions—whether to be a missionary halfway across the world or to deal drugs—our responses lay either one more block in the wall dividing us or one more brick in the bridge uniting us. I pray at least one family's story will encourage and help you as you show your child *love no matter what.*

1

Who Are You, and What Have You Done with My Child?

The Decisions Parents Don't Want to Make

How did you know you could go home and your parents wouldn't say, 'I told you so'?" I asked my dear, thirtyish friend. My friend had been the proverbial wild child during her graduate school years. Her relationship with her parents during that time was almost nonexistent due to her anger toward them.

"I just knew," she confidently answered.

I just knew. Her statement stuck in my heart. Little did I know then that it would become the mantra for my parenting.

Several years later our eighteen-year-old daughter, Katie, called an impromptu meeting with Gene and me.

"Mom, Dad," she announced, "I'm moving out next weekend." Her words shocked me to the point of numbness.

The past couple of years had been a struggle with Katie. Every day brought on one form of rebellion or another, all against our authority as parents, with her becoming upset about something. Rarely did she do as she was asked without a bad attitude. I used to say, "If Katie's in the house, it's rockin'," because she thrived on stirring up everyone. She clung to her friends—not unusual behavior for a child her age—but these were friends who were bad for her. Tensions escalated after high school. She went through life with a storm cloud over her.

Her rebellion finally caused her to feel she could live under our roof no longer. She told us she had been looking for apartments for a while and had found one. But this was not a wise time for her to leave. Katie was not even a year out of high school. She made only minimum wage at a part-time job while she attended community college. She obviously did not make enough to support herself, let alone pay for college, so why move ten minutes away to live on her own without enough money to pay her bills? Though she was old enough to be on her own, she was not in a good financial or even emotional state. Her choice to move out was a decision we did not agree with.

She continued to surprise us. "Mark and his friends will move me out on Saturday," she declared. Mark was her boyfriend at the time. He implied that he was a Christian, but his life said otherwise. He was a push-it-to-the-limit-and-then-some troubled kid. Many were the stories of his adventures. Other people warned us of his past actions and the consequences he faced. Katie didn't say they would be living together, but we didn't trust Mark not to take advantage of the situation.

This move was not the beginning of a parade of Katie's decisions that Gene and I didn't agree with, nor would it be the last. She next asked us to give her the money we had set aside as her four-year college money in order to pay her living expenses until she was promoted to a full-time position. Katie was close to finishing community college and heading off to a four-year college, but she wanted to gamble her savings on the chance she would receive the full-time position! While we could have withheld the money, Gene and I realized it would have been a moot point. It was time for Katie to learn some hard lessons and for us to let her go—college money included.

Our angst was not because our daughter was moving out and pursuing her independent life (we wanted that!). Our angst was grounded in the reality that she was moving out in anger, without a means of supporting herself, and for the reason of instant gratification. And on top of that, she was not moving out to go to college, to start a career, or to get married. We would have been supportive and excited for any of these situations. She was moving out in a huff without considering the consequences. She was in total rebellion, and because of anger and immaturity, she was derailing her plan for college and a career she loved. Mark would now be her new ally, and we certainly did not trust him.

Of course I did not want strange boys coming into my home and taking my daughter's possessions to who-knows-where. But I'm grateful that right then God alerted me to be quiet and reminded me that the wrong words spoken in the heat of the moment would seriously cripple any influence I had left in her life. I sat silently as Gene calmly asked for more information about her plans. The reality that our lives would never be the same sank into my heart. Our daughter was walking out, and she didn't care how loudly the door slammed behind her. She was not asking for our blessing or even our advice about her plan. She was *telling* us what was happening—with or without our help. Her plans were not up for discussion, even though we tried to reason with her.

Gene and I needed a response to our daughter that would not build walls but a bridge. Our response needed to be about her and what was truly best for her, not about our hurt feelings, anger, or disappointment. We told her we would help. Gene began to plan how many pickup loads it would take to move her few belongings. In the next couple of days I went through the house finding extra household items—casserole dishes, towels, pans, linens. At one time we owned a small motor home camper. I had kept the items from the kitchen and the bed and bath linens, so I had most of the basics she needed to stock her apartment.

Katie has always been a strong-willed girl. Throughout her childhood I often struggled to know how to be the mom she needed. She has a tender heart, loves to laugh, and is an incredibly talented artist. She loves to make and give thoughtful, creative gifts (including the wrappings). She is the best friend anyone could ask for. She is an absolute to delight to me.

I have a vivid memory of her kindergarten picture: Katie is wearing a pastel pink dress with an opaque white ruffled collar. Her curly red hair is in a French-braided ponytail with flyaway strands everywhere, as it was a hot and humid day when the picture was taken. In my mind's eye, that little girl still is and has always been my Katie.

Katie is an artist. Her creative personality makes her even more sensitive to her surroundings, others' interactions with her, and her own physical feelings. Katie recently shared with me that all this, coupled with the frustration of not knowing how to express her creativity, often came out in a disagreeable personality or behavior. She often responded with anger, frustration, and bad moods. Since my personality is very different, I had no clue about what she was going through or the frustration she felt. My personality is more a let's-figure-out-the-problem-and-fix-it type. So of course, my natural way of responding did not help Katie. I wanted to fix her, but she didn't need fixing. She needed to be heard and understood and then guided and encouraged in the unique journey God created her to fulfill.

Katie's Thoughts

Communicating with your children about their thought processes and their decision making is so important. Sometimes we kids don't even know why we are doing what we are doing. Talking things out in a calm, safe environment helps parents and kids think things through.

My mom told me a couple of years ago that when I felt overwhelmed in social situations, I should stop and think about what specifically was upsetting me. That technique has helped me in school, work, and relationships. I wouldn't have thought of that unless my mom and I were having a conversation about my actions and how they affected me and others.

Junior high was even more difficult for Katie because, as all moms know, junior high girls can be mean. A couple of years ago one of Katie's friends shared a story with her from their junior high days. Two of the most popular girls asked Katie's friend to walk with them past the edge of the school playground where no one was around. She went with them because she was eager to be accepted by these girls. Once out of earshot of the other kids and the teacher on duty, the girls told Katie's friend, "No one likes you. You have no friends." Katie's friend was crushed and too embarrassed to share it with anyone until she and Katie were twenty-three.

Katie was shocked—the girls did the same exact thing to her. She too had told no one (not even me). But the poison of this lie had eaten at both girls' self-esteem for over a decade, during some of their most formative years. No wonder Katie came home from school in a huff and a thundercloud covered the house once she walked in! School was a jungle for her, and she didn't know how to express it to us.

In senior high Katie decided she would no longer be the victim. She made friends who were not good for her and who encouraged her to challenge Gene's and my boundaries and rules. Oh boy, high school was hard on all of us. One boy who befriended her, Austin, also secretly spread mean rumors about her. Then when she was hurt she went running back to him for comfort. It was his vicious cycle to keep Katie's attention at her own costly expense. Gene and I knew this boy was not good for her, but the more we tried to warn her and put up boundaries, the harder she worked to be with him.

Can you relate? I bet you can. It's hard, isn't it? It's hard to believe that our kids and our relationships with them could ever change. We think

- we will always know our kids better than anyone.
- we will always enjoy the same closeness as when we rocked them in our laps.

- they will always run to us with their hurts like they did when they were little.
- they will always trust what we say over what anyone else says.
- the child in the kindergarten picture will seamlessly mature into an adult version of herself, and we will live happily ever after as one big family.

Screech! Stop. Why do we believe that? Why do we think our family will be the first to mature without any bumps or bruises along the way? Likely most of us can think of *one* family where it appears everyone is living emotionally and spiritually healthy lives. And maybe they are. If so, I am extremely happy for them. Really, I am. But for the rest of us, why do we believe the fairy tale of happily ever after?

I believe it is because in part, and without directly saying so, the modern American Christian community made an unrealistic promise to parents. It goes something like this: if you raise your kids exactly how we say, applying all you learn in sermons, Sunday school, Christian radio, podcasts—and don't forget all those Christian books (like this one!)—then your child will turn out perfectly. If, however, you make one mistake, the promise is null and void. You will have failed as a parent.

I know that sounds harsh. And I know that is *not* what the Christian community meant to say. But it is what many of us Christian parents heard. I know. I'm one of them. I tried to do all I could, but I couldn't do it all. My kids aren't perfect. (And neither am I.)

Let's do a reality check here. We'll start with the Bible. Go ahead and open your Bible to page 2 (or maybe page 3). Start where it says, "When the woman saw that the fruit of the tree was good for food and pleasing to the eye, and also desirable for gaining wisdom, she took some and ate it" (Genesis 3:6 NIV). The woman is Eve. Her Father is the Creator of everything—God almighty. We don't know exactly how old Eve is when this happens, but it is early in God's parenting. In only a short amount of time since being created as God's child, Eve does the one thing He told her not to do. In doing so she brings into play sin and its consequences for the entire human race.

Many in today's Christian community might imply that if only God had parented better He would have known what Eve was up to and could have prevented it. You know, God did know what Eve was up to, yet He allowed it. Eve listened to the serpent, believed his lies, disbelieved God's promise, gave into the lust of her eyes, and ate the fruit! Does that make God a bad parent? We all know this one—no, of course not! Did Eve's disobedience catch God off-guard? Again—no, of course not. So why are we surprised when our kids (or other people's kids) make decisions we don't agree with? Why are we so hard on our kids and ourselves?

Kids have been making decisions their parents don't agree since the original First Family.

Go back to Genesis 3 in your Bible and read a little farther down the page. See the part about the brothers, Cain and Abel, in chapter 4? These two are the second generation from the hand of God, and they can't get along—so much so that Cain kills his brother. And so goes the early history of man—constantly disobeying our Creator and heavenly Father. Yet God never hides His face in embarrassment. He understands who we are and loves us in a way that keeps the door open to a relationship with Him, while neither approving of nor winking at our sin.

We love our kids so much, but for whatever reason they won't listen to us. They move headlong into doing life their way, and their decisions don't make sense to us.

Jan and George's son, David, also made decisions they didn't agree with. Junior high was difficult for David. He was eventually diagnosed with ADD and put on medication, but his attitude didn't improve. He became more defiant. When he was a freshman in high school, Jan received a call from the mom of one of David's friends. David was smoking marijuana with her son. And so began David's parade of decisions Jan and George didn't understand. His grades continued to decline. After David admitted he was depressed, Jan took him to a Christian counselor. He was put on medication for depression, but his behavior became more bizarre and angry.

A few weeks later David snuck out at night to drink alcohol and smoke marijuana with friends. He came back to the house and took his parents' van—even though he did not yet have a driver's license—to drive friends to get something to eat. He crashed the van. No one was seriously hurt, but it was a major turning point for everyone. Jan said, "David said the accident made him worse—he sank deeper in shame and guilt."

Jan and George were clueless as to why David was behaving this way. They had done their best to raise him in a caring Christian home. They had modeled love, respect, and faithfulness in their marriage. Their younger daughter was doing well

academically, socially, and spiritually. Why was David struggling?
Had they done something wrong?

Gene and I have felt that way about Katie too. She seemed to have
lost her way. Dealing with mean kids, making college and career
decisions, keeping up with schoolwork, and trying to find God
in all of the chaos—together it was almost too much for her to
process.

When our kids bounce from one poor decision to the next,
often they are not ready or able to deal with all the stimuli coming
into their brains. While our kids may look like adults, their brains
still have much developing to do before they are mature enough
to make well-informed decisions. According to literature from the
US Department of Health and Human Services, "The prefrontal
cortex takes in information from all of the senses and orchestrates
thoughts and actions to achieve specific goals." The literature goes
on to say that this part of the brain is "one of the last regions of the
brain to reach maturation." The prefrontal cortex's jobs include
"focusing attention," "organizing thoughts and problem solving,"
"foreseeing and weighing possible consequences of behavior," and
"modulation of intense emotions." This part of the brain is not
completely developed until about the age of 25.[1]

Even if our kids are taller than we are, many times they reason
more like the kindergarteners in the pictures in our scrapbooks.
And this is the challenge for parents. As our kids grow older, they
are given more freedom and privileges by the law and by school;
even churches often assign more responsibilities and leadership
roles to teens who appear to be mature Christian kids. However,

on the inside they are teetering between childhood and adulthood. We have no warning to know when they're operating from their childlike brains or their adult brains.

Add to all this the messiness of their peers and the possibility that some of their coaches, teachers, or other adults in their lives are not emotionally and spiritually mature—is it any wonder our kids sometimes make decisions we don't agree with?

Sadly, church was not a safe place for Katie to process all this. (I'm not beating up on the church in general; it was just the reality of our specific situation.) She had one good friend in her youth group. After that friend moved out of the area, she was left with girls in our church's youth group who were not kind to her.

Lisa and James's son, Greg, also did not fit in with his youth group. He struggled with self-esteem issues during his growing-up years and had difficulty feeling like part of the group. Lisa explains, "Something happened with one of the kids and he would not go back." Wow. One situation with one kid can make such a difference.

Again, I am not bashing the church. My goal is to help us understand, even a little, what our teens and young adult kids go through. These challenging situations would be hard for us and are even harder for our kids since their prefrontal cortexes are not fully mature. Yes, our kids do and will continue to make decisions we don't agree with, but often they are doing the best they can with their circumstances and reasoning ability.

But as parents often struggle to respond well when their kids make decisions they don't agree with, the church, too, struggles to respond in love when kids don't fit into the expected "Christian kid" mold.

In his book *The Last Christian Generation*, Josh McDowell states "various denomination leaders" have shared with him their estimates that "between sixty-nine percent (69%) and ninety-four percent (94%) of their young people are leaving the traditional church after high school . . . and very few are returning."[2] Consider the youth group in your church. McDowell also quotes from George Barna's book *Real Teens*: "Now only thirty-three percent (33%) of churched youth say that,"[3] suggesting that only one-third of those kids will be in church in the next four years. Since our kids make up the youth group, we must be alert to the possibility that they may or may not choose to attend church after they leave home. I'm not saying this will be the case in your home, but these statistics alert us to the trend in the American body of Christ. *Our* kids *will* make decisions we don't agree with.

In Luke 15:11–32 Jesus tells a parable about a son who made many decisions his father didn't agree with. We will unpack this parable through this book, but for now let's consider only verse 13: "And not many days later, the younger son gathered everything together and went on a journey into a distant country, and there he squandered his estate with loose living" (NASB). Sometimes kids pack up and move to the "distant country," and we don't know what they're up to. This is the trying part for many parents. But when our kids are teens and young adults, often they are still in the home or living nearby when they are making decisions we don't agree with. We see them frequently. We hear about their latest adventures. The neighbors hear. The church hears. Life becomes even more complicated.

Our goal is to become like the father in the parable. Verse 20 says, "But while he was still a long way off, his father saw him and felt compassion for him, and ran and embraced him and kissed him" (NASB). The phrase *long way off* means "at a distance . . . [implying] a road, journey or highway."[4] The son was on his way back, but still a long way from home, when "his father saw him." *Saw* means "to know, be aware, perceive."[5] Remember when your kids were young? You always kept your ears on alert so you could sense where they were—you could tell if they were in the bedroom playing or if they moved to the family room to watch a video. Maybe it became too quiet and you found them coloring the tiles around the bathtub. It's parents' intuition. The father in the parable kept his senses alert to his wayward son. He was on the lookout for news about him or even for the sight of him coming home. So while the son was on his way back, before the father even knew the son was coming, he saw his son. His heart was open toward his son. He was ready for his son's return, and he ran to embrace him.

Our goal is to keep our hearts open toward our children so we can do whatever we are called upon to do for their benefit— whatever says to them, *I love you no matter what*. This will not always be our first reaction. It is hard to show love, especially if our kids are making immoral decisions or ones with legal consequences. As we journey together we'll learn to adjust to our new reality and to speak love in a way that does not encourage or embrace their sin but allows us to embrace our kids. Together we will walk through our confusion, hurt, disappointment, anger, or embarrassment to arrive at a place of compassion, forgiveness, and relationship with our children.

For the past two to three years I have been speaking to and

talking with parents about the topic of children making decisions we don't agree with. I wish you could see the faces of the parents who, after I've shared about this topic, have told their stories as if I were their most trusted friend. Over and over again, I have had this experience—talking with guests in my home, with friends of friends, with business associates, with people I run into everywhere I go.

We may not share our stories with those in our circles of influence, but given the opportunity to share with someone who is walking a similar journey and is crazy enough to tell her story, we find that the words and emotions flow freely. I believe it is healing and comforting for us to experience acceptance and understanding for our situations and our children. It is a gift we can give each other as we struggle to know what to do when our kids make decisions we don't agree with and we work to show them that we love them no matter what.

2

What Exactly Are We Talking About?

Types of Decisions We Disagree With

Katie's decision to move out at that specific time was not the wisest one. She had no way to support herself. In fact, part of her plan was to use some of her college money to pay the bills until she was accepted for a full-time job. But she didn't care about any of these obstacles. Her goal was to get out of our home and on her own. She didn't care that her decision was derailing the original plan of staying under the umbrella of our home—a situation that provided everything she needed, including health insurance—until she was ready to transfer to a four-year college to finish her degree. Then she would be in a good position to move out and start her own life. No, she wanted to move out right then and was willing to sacrifice all her efforts and assets to make it happen.

However, Katie's decision to move out was not the end of

the world, and our response needed to be appropriate, not melo-
dramatic. My husband's initial response was much different than
mine. Gene recalls, "By then I was expecting it, because she was
so hard to get along with. My knee-jerk reaction was, *Great! What
a relief!*" His second thought was more fatherly: "I knew the only
way I could help her was to let her go out and try. We weren't
going to argue her out of it."

I, too, had the same type of prompting from God. From
this point forward life would be Katie's best teacher. She was
done listening to us—for a while. It would be her and God
alone now.

Katie's decision wasn't wrong morally or legally. It was immature. As parents we need to gain perspective on our children's
decisions by analyzing what types of decisions they are making.
Let's look at the four types of decisions our kids make.

Decisions That Are Truly Preferences

I don't know how to say this without offending someone, so I'll
just say it: some parents make issues out of nothing. One child
chooses a different college than the one his parent *prefers*, so
the parent becomes angry or distant. Another child chooses an
extracurricular activity different from the one her parent *prefers*;
for example, the teen daughter prefers forensics or the chemistry
club to cheerleading, and her former-cheerleader mom over-
reacts because her daughter is not following in her footsteps.
So the parent begins a campaign to try to convince the child to
choose differently.

Believe me, I know from personal experience the temptation

to overreact when my child chooses a preference different from mine. Skim through my first book, *Queen Mom*[1], and you'll get a little glimpse of the ugliness when my control-freak, monster-mom head reared itself. But I thought I was right. I actually thought it was wrong (or at least not proper) for my fifth-grade daughter to wear her shirt untucked. (In my defense, in the early nineties it was the style to tuck in shirts.) Of course, I made a big deal about it.

My most memorable and painful experience of overreacting was caught on videotape, and I was the one taping it! Every year the girls and I decorated Christmas cookies. I set up the video camera with the kitchen table and the girls (ages ten, eight, and three) around it in view. Then I let the camera roll. Oh my word! I am sad to recall what a control freak I was. I wanted obedient girls and a mess-free experience. I can hear you laughing. Christmas cookie decorating with little girls is never mess free and is certainly not the time for prim and proper manners. It should be a time filled with silliness and giggles. My tension was revealed in my staccato tone and impatience with the girls not getting it "right." Even now I can remember how tense I was because things were not going according to my preference. For the record, the girls love this tape. They say they can't tell I'm upset, but I know I am. I know it affected our day together. And why? Because I couldn't loosen up over cookie dough and frosting.

You may be thinking, *Christmas cookie decorating is nothing compared to the life decisions my child is making.* And you're right. But my point is this—if our attitude says our way is the only way, we are damaging our relationships with our children no matter whether we are talking about Christmas cookies or college. Are you willing to risk your relationship with your child over your preference?

Donna and Bob almost risked their relationship with their daughter, Allison, when Allison started seriously dating a young man, Thomas. He was nothing like the man they thought she would fall in love with. Bob and Donna saw many red flags even at the beginning of the relationship. He professed to be a Christian, but Bob and Donna did not see evidence in his life to support his claim. This was a major red flag for them. Thomas treated Allison well, but he tended to be possessive. "His possessiveness scared me," Connie says. Thomas had a job, but not one that could support them. At gatherings at Bob and Donna's house, he sat alone and did not join in the conversations even when included. It was more than awkward shyness. His demeanor seemed to say, "I don't like you and I don't care if you like me." He was only interested in Allison and his few friends from work.

Donna and Bob shared their concerns with Allison—in fact, they now feel they shared too many concerns. But Allison was a strong-willed girl, and she would not listen. In a few months Allison and Thomas were engaged. Bob and Donna had to decide how to proceed. Allison seemed bent on marrying Thomas, and nothing they said seemed to have an effect on her.

Bob and Donna had done all the "right" things Christian parents are supposed to do—they brought her up in the church, helped her memorize scripture, went on the mother-daughter purity weekend, and even relocated when Allison was in junior high so she could attend a Christian school and get away from negative influences. But none of these things seemed to matter: Allison was determined to do life her way. Regarding the marriage, Donna says, "I was shocked she chose to marry someone almost a direct opposite of her dad. But we couldn't have done anything differently to cause her to make a different decision."

So with a wedding to plan, Bob and Donna knew they either could get on board or risk losing their relationship with Allison. They decided to pursue a relationship with their son-in-law-to-be. They gave their daughter a beautiful wedding. They did all they could to encourage a healthy marriage. Please note here: Allison's choice was a preference issue. Bob and Donna did not have reason to believe her safety was at risk.

Now Donna and Allison enjoy the best relationship they have ever had. "Through her whole life we have shown her unconditional love. She knows we love her no matter what," Donna says.

A preference is just that—choosing one thing over another. It's not right, wrong, or foolish, but it might be a different decision than the one we would make. But many parents see their kids' decisions as right or wrong, good or bad. The key in discerning a preference is seeing if there is any absolute right or wrong in the decision.

Other examples of preferences are the many choices of body "enhancements" that often cause conflict. These include unusual hair dyes, body piercings, and tattoos. I am not in favor of any of these—but I'm also not willing for them to be an obstacle between my children and me. Our girls all have beautiful red or strawberry blonde hair (I'm not biased; just stating the facts). Yet they have found the need to streak it with various colors—purple triumphed as the favorite. Do I like it? No. Do they know I don't like it? I've mentioned it once or twice. But there are so many other more important issues in their lives I want to have input into that I choose to look past the purple streaks. If I make purple hair an issue, I become background noise in their lives. I didn't come this far as a mom to become background noise.

I realize body piercings and tattoos have far-reaching consequences. Some cross into the "foolish" category. My friend and fellow author Jess MacCallum had to decide how to handle the tattoo question with his teen son. I'll let Jess tell his story.

"Kyle, now twenty, began bugging me about a tattoo when he was sixteen and playing in a 'metal' band. I told him that a tattoo was the birthmark of a fool. That didn't slow him down, and with his generation roaring ahead with 'body art' I began to wonder if I could do something that would make use of this rather than [let it become] a point of conflict. Despite some interpretations of certain Old Testament passages that imply tattoos are a pagan thing to do, I saw [them] as a purely cultural expression, [which] could only be limited by personal preference and common sense. And that means being flexible if Kyle disagreed with me when he turned eighteen and could legally do what he wanted. Of course, I could always play the 'not under my roof' card, but how much does that really accomplish if you use it all the time? And doesn't that just pull the arrow back farther and release farther when they do eventually leave?

"So I decided to make him a deal: we'd both get the same tattoo if I could pick it out. And I'd pay for it as his birthday present. He was hesitant until I said the only thing I'd want was our Scottish family crest. He was thrilled, being equally proud of his heritage, and I let him pick his left shoulder or left back over his heart. I chose a traditional black version on the shoulder; he picked full color on his back. We made an event of it, and even the artist had never had something like that happen.

"I still limit his tattooing while he is under my roof—no hands, neck, face; no quick decisions or impulsive designs. Recently, my oldest daughter turned eighteen. Having set the pattern with her brother, I was obligated to follow through or be labeled 'unfair.' So she and my wife got modest, meaningful tattoos together and bonded in the way my son and I had. I think my wife and I are done for now, since our other daughter is just fourteen and not the tattoo type. I can't help but wonder what will be in vogue in four years.

"By the way, when my seventy-seven-year-old mother grimaced at my tattoo, I told her not to worry; it was only temporary. It couldn't last more than about forty to fifty years at this point."

Body enhancements are viewed with a wide range of opinions in the body of Christ. Believers who I never imagined would have approved of tattoos, much less have a tattoo, have surprised me when their body art has caught me unawares. I do not take body enhancements lightly. Parents need to seek God and discern what is best for each kid in each situation. Sometimes that means we will use the "not under my roof" reason, and we will appear unfair.

Decisions That Seem Foolish

Katie's decision to move out seemed foolish. She would not heed our concerns. It seemed absurd to us that she would spend her college money to live only a few miles away in a mediocre apartment when she had everything she could want here in our home. But she was determined to persevere in her foolishness.

The Bible defines *foolish* as "stupid or silly,"[2] or "heedless, blockhead [yep, that's in the Bible dictionary], absurd."[3] Many of the decisions our kids make will be foolish. Everyone but the child sees the ridiculousness of the decision. Proverbs 22:15 says, "Foolishness is bound up in the heart of a child." *Foolishness*, then, can be defined as "silliness." As the parents of three daughters, Gene and I have experienced lots of silliness. Sometimes we observe it and sometimes we join in with it. But the silliness described in the above verse is not good-natured fun. The silliness talked about here is *folly*, which is defined as "lack of understanding or sense . . . costly and foolish undertaking."[5]

We need to expect our kids to make foolish decisions just as we need to expect them to make decisions that are not in line with our preferences. They are their own people with their individual personalities, wills, talents, interests, likes, dislikes, and so on. We are the foolish ones if we expect them to always make the same choices we do or to make good choices all the time.

Julie and Marty couldn't have been more shocked by their son's foolishness. Aaron is a "good kid." For the most part he did what his parents asked. But in high school he felt he didn't fit in at youth group. He went to church out of obedience, but he wasn't invested as his parents were. After graduation he agreed to go to college. Marty and Julie were blessed financially, so they paid for him to go to a good university. In his junior year Aaron dropped a couple of classes, and he continued to drop some each semester until he didn't enroll at all in his final semester. The bigger problem was that he didn't tell his parents but kept taking their checks for tuition and room and board. He stayed at school but didn't attend classes. Julie said, "It should have clicked, but it didn't." He used some of the money for living expenses but didn't spend more than he needed.

Aaron made foolish choices—dropping out of school and lying to his family. Like many kids he felt stuck. He didn't want to disappoint his parents, but he didn't feel college was for him. He didn't have a plan B. His immature reasoning skills kicked in and out popped foolishness.

Decisions That Are Immoral or Illegal

After a few months in her first apartment, Katie informed Gene and me that she and her boyfriend, Mark, would be sharing an apartment—with two bedrooms. She swore nothing was going on, but to Gene and me this was an immoral decision. Once again we were faced with the dilemma of wanting to nurture our relationship with our daughter while not in agreement with her decision. Our response needed to be wrapped in love and biblically based. We decided that this meant we would not visit their apartment, but both of them were always welcome in our home.

However, identifying moral decisions is not so easy and can be a matter of interpretation. Parents need to proceed carefully when applying labels to their kids' decisions. Most Christians would agree that we are God's temple, as stated in 1 Corinthians 6:19: "Do you not know that your bodies are temples of the Holy Spirit, who is in you, whom you have received from God? You are not your own" (UPDATED NIV). But the rub comes in verse 20: "You were bought at a price. Therefore honor God with your bodies" (UPDATED NIV). Herein lies the messy debate of how we honor God with our bodies.

The general consensus among believers is that smoking is wrong because it kills our bodies, which are God's temple. And they are right. However, many of that same group of believers wink at the obesity that is prevalent not only in our society but in the body of Christ. Heart disease is the number one killer of men and women in the United States.[6] The Centers for Disease Control and Prevention states, "High cholesterol, high blood pressure, obesity, diabetes, tobacco use, unhealthy diet, physical inactivity, and secondhand smoke are also risk factors associated with heart disease."[7] Most, if not all, of these risk factors can be controlled or affected by the way we live and take care of ourselves. Yet many believers do not take care of their bodies, nor do they consider this neglect to be sinful.

A few years ago a couple of college girls from the Netherlands' Youth for Christ visited our little town. One day they gave a presentation to our community's Bible study. They shared how Christian culture in America differs from that in the Netherlands. We were surprised to learn that the believers in the Netherlands find fast food sinful because it is so bad for our bodies—the temple of God. Our group looked at each other in disbelief and with a little shame. Fast food was a way of life for most of us and our families. What one part of the body of Christ considered no big deal, another part of the body considered sin.

The way we take care of our bodies is only one area where we parents may be hypocritical in our interpretation of the Bible's stance on morality. If we want to make a big deal about the way our kids are taking care of their bodies (smoking tobacco or marijuana, drinking, tattoos, piercings), we need to hold the magnifying glass to ourselves first and make sure we are caring well for our temples.

Often we parents climb to our moral high ground on the backs of our own moral discrepancies. If I wanted to meddle, I would mention your entertainment choices, your participation in pornography or an affair, or your lack of integrity in business or on your taxes. The list could go on, but you get the idea. None of us is perfect. However, most teens are highly alert to hypocrisy, and that is one of the main reasons kids stop listening to their parents. Before we tear into our kids for their immoral choices, we need to look at our own and clean up our lives. Then with grace, humility, and love we will be ready to pursue a relationship with and guide our children.

In Matthew 7:1–5 Jesus speaks pointedly to our tendency to claim moral high ground over someone else while having our own issues. He starts by saying, "Judge not, that you be not judged." Here, *judge* means "decide (morally or judicially) . . . to try; condemn."[8] Jesus tells us not to be the judge, not to try a person (or his actions) and judge against him. It's not our job. If we want a voice in our kids' lives, we need to remember our own sinfulness and wear the humility and love of Christ at all times (Matthew 11:29; 2 Corinthians 10:1).

Yes, we are to discern the truth. Hebrews 5:14 says, "But solid food is for the mature, who because of practice have their senses trained to discern good and evil" (NASB). Discerning good from evil comes from spiritual maturity, which includes humility and the love of God. We are not to be critical in our discerning but remember we all fall short of God's plan for us

(Romans 3:23). We will see in coming chapters the harmful effects of a critical attitude. Right now, let's allow our attitudes toward our kids and their decisions to marinate in God's grace and mercy toward us.

God's grace and mercy are what Cynthia and Frank needed desperately for themselves and their daughter, Andrea. Cynthia shares, "Frank and I had a difficult marriage at the start. We were not in church, and I was pregnant with Andrea." During the first six to seven years of their marriage, Cynthia and Frank separated several times, and they moved often in the first five years. During Andrea's childhood Cynthia and Andrea enjoyed a close relationship, but Frank and Andrea did not get along. Frank's and Andrea's personalities were similar, and Frank was, according to Cynthia, a "controlling person," which further fed the tension in their relationship.

Once she was in college, Andrea's attitude toward her mom began to change. She became very closed off, and if Cynthia asked her a question, she would become defensive. One weekend Cynthia visited Andrea at college. During that visit Andrea told Cynthia she was gay. The turning point for Andrea was the upperclassman mentor assigned to her through her athletic team. The mentor was a lesbian and was the final push Andrea needed to make that lifestyle choice. They moved in together soon after.

In that initial conversation with Andrea, Cynthia's instinct was to protect her daughter and make everything all right. She responded, "You will pack your bags and you will come home with me this evening." Of course, that didn't happen. "On the drive home I was screaming and yelling and crying. I cried out to God, 'This can't be,'" Cynthia recalls. In one moment, many of Cynthia's hopes and dreams for her daughter and her family were gone. There would be no son-in-law or grandkids. From this point forward life as they imagined it was no more. Frank and Cynthia began the process of dealing with their own emotions and thinking through how to respond to Andrea's immoral lifestyle—all the while keeping and healing their relationship with their daughter.

The messiness of our kids' decisions often smears the lines between foolish, immoral, and illegal into one murky mess. Robert and Connie returned home unexpectedly early one evening to find their son Jeremy hosting friends (against the rules when parents weren't home) for a pot-smoking party (not only against house rules but against the law!). They sent the other boys home, and the following day they called the boys' parents. Many parents would not believe that their sons were involved. Next Robert called the local police—not for legal action but for a "scared straight" experience for his son. Robert talked to the police officer once in person and twice on the phone over a two-week period. He was told an officer would chat with Jeremy to make him think twice about drug use, but the department never followed through. Even though Jeremy made an illegal choice, the local law enforcement treated it as something for the parents to deal with.

Drug use is illegal. But prosecuting marijuana use is not always at the top of the police's priority list, so by default it falls to the parents to enforce the rules. Robert and Connie accepted the reality that Jeremy was regularly using marijuana. They continued to show him love while working on a plan to deal with his poor choice.

Decisions to Get Out of God's Way

Lisa and James (from chapter 1) found themselves where they never guessed they would be—letting their son face prison time. Greg continued down the slippery slope after not finding a place in high school or youth group. He became a regular user of drugs and alcohol. At age twenty-nine he was arrested for possession of cocaine. The judge gave him many chances to get his life in order. After his last arrest the judge gave him one more chance to walk away with a fairly clean record. All Greg needed to do was to show up in court, finish paying his fines, and complete community service, and the felony would not be on his record. He would have the opportunity to find a job and move on with his life.

But Greg purposefully missed the court date, giving the excuse that he didn't get the notice (one of many previously sent to him). James and Lisa could have picked him up and taken him to court. But after sixteen years, it was time for Greg to take ownership of his life and decisions. His parents let the court system be his teacher. No one wants to see his child lose his his driver's license or go to jail, but we must remember our heavenly Father loves our kids more than we do. He will do whatever He needs to bring your lost sheep to Himself.

In Luke 15:4–7, Jesus tells the story of the man who leaves his ninety-nine sheep grazing to look for the one lost sheep. He explains how the man responds when he finds the lost one: "And when he comes home, he calls together his friends and his neighbors, saying to them, 'Rejoice with me, for I have found my sheep which was lost!'" (v. 6 NASB). He goes on: "I tell you that in the same way, there will be more joy in heaven over one sinner who repents than over ninety-nine righteous persons who need no repentance" (v. 7). Can you feel the heart of God—how deeply He yearns for *your lost sheep to come to Him*? Notice in the story the sheep is away from the others. He is alone and on his own. It is in this lonely place the shepherd finds him and brings him back. We will talk about this more, but start realizing that for many of our kids this is *the only place they can hear the voice of the Shepherd*. They must get away from our voices—whether we are speaking too much or not. They must be in a place where they hear only the voice of the Shepherd. We have become a buffer between them and God, so we need to be out of the way.

We don't know where our children will hear the voice of the Shepherd. Are we willing to let God work and not try to prevent God's hand moving in their lives? Prison may just be the place God gets the attention of your child.

George and Jan (from chapter 1) also let the legal system work in the life of their son, David. After difficult junior high years and with no positive change after tenth grade, they found a Christian ranch home where David could live during the school year. The boys at the ranch study academics and improve their spiritual lives as well as build character while working the ranch. David was accepted to the program. After several weeks he was allowed to come home for a few days. When it was time for him to return to the ranch, he didn't want to go. He became too violent for George and the two grandfathers as they tried to put him in the car, so they called the police, who came and handcuffed him. They gave him the choice to go to jail or back to the ranch. He chose to go back.

Many parents may feel it would be too humiliating for the neighbors to see the police at their house and watch the struggle between their child, their family, and the police, but it was what was best for David.

Let's stop here and examine our perspective. We say our kids come first, but do they? What is worth more to you—your reputation with your neighbor or your child's best interest? What is more important—the appearance of normalcy or your child getting the help he needs?

One of the most difficult changes parents need to make so they can *love their children no matter what* is to gain proper perspective on what's important and for eternity, versus what's for appearances and will be gone in a breath.

As I said in chapter 1, the more I share on this topic the more convinced I am that we are the silent majority. I believe there are more families trying to discern how to respond when their kids make decisions they don't agree with than there are families where there seems to be not a hiccup. We are in this together. I'll let my daughter Katie close this chapter.

Katie's Thoughts

When parents and kids disagree, it sets up a dynamic that makes it impossible for either side to win or even find something to feel good about together. It's hard to forget your parents telling you something like "you will fail," even if the decisions aren't going to work out anyway. When they don't and you know that your parents knew all along, it just makes the situation worse. Now you know that you made a bad decision, and you not only have to suffer the consequences but to give your parents credit for calling it before it happened. Even if your parents don't say, "I told you so," they're thinking it. And you know that they're thinking it.

The only thing kids need to know is that their parents either agree or don't agree with their decisions. We don't need a fortune-teller or other critical judgments. Let us figure out how it will end for us. If it doesn't work, we need your support and advice for the future—not a Monday morning quarterback to make us feel even worse for our lack of foresight.

Constant support can be hard. I know it is hard for my parents to keep watching me take a path they wouldn't.

3

It Is Not All About You

Getting Your Sorry Self Out of the Way

I was clueless when I was pregnant with my firstborn. It didn't occur to me to read a parenting book. I'm sure many of you can relate. When we left the hospital with our baby, I know we weren't thinking past surviving the next few days. In those first few weeks we focused on doing the next thing and catching a few hours of sleep if possible. Unfortunately for most parents, operating day-to-day becomes the norm as the kids grow into their elementary school years—we keep doing the next thing and grab what sleep we can. By the time I had my second child, the book *What to Expect When You're Expecting*[1] was in bookstores (you remember—those buildings you visited where you could actually hold the book before you purchased it?). I remember chuckling as my sister devoured it during her first pregnancy. I thought, *If I don't know it now I never will*. But what do I know? At the time of this writing, that book is rated number one in Amazon's pregnancy and childbirth category. Apparently lots of parents bought it.

Unfortunately, more parents buy books on what to expect in pregnancy than books on what to do when their kids hit the junior high years and beyond and start making choices they don't agree with. Few parents plan for the worst—or not even the worst, but a variance from their assumed, yet unspoken, plans for their kids. You did not dream that your kids would veer from your plan. The reality is, they will.

You haven't allowed yourselves to peek behind that door of their future—the one labeled *Not What I Expected When I Was Expecting*. Even though the alarm on this door occasionally goes off, you have managed to ignore it and keep the door locked—or so you thought.

Now the day has come. Your child picked the lock and is rummaging through the scenarios of what you never expected, deciding which ones she will try on first. But since you never considered the possibility of your child's exploration of what's behind this door, you are unprepared for her choices.

Because of your unpreparedness, your reactions to her decisions say to her, "It's all about me!" You tell her

- how put out you are.
- how inconvenienced you are.
- how disappointed you are.
- how embarrassed you are.
- how hurt you are.

The reality is, *it's not all about you!* It's all about your child, and you need to get your sorry self out of the way. Yes, you need to deal with the situation wisely and in a helpful fashion, but you are not the issue. Your child is the issue. She is front and center.

By making yourself the issue, you further distance yourself from your child and lessen your chances of being heard.

Wrong Motives for Parents

When you make yourself the primary issue, you are reacting from wrong motives instead of considering what is best for your child. Your wrong motives might include some of the following:

- Pride—you want to keep your reputation and your child's reputation intact.
- Your expectations—you want your dreams for your child fulfilled, especially since you know best.
- Your needs—you want everything to stay the same so your needs will continue to be met through your relationship with your child.
- Selfishness—you want to parent the way you always have. You don't want to find new ways to effectively reach your child.
- Comfort—you don't want your child to venture where you yourself are uncomfortable.

I understand these motives. I know the pain of a child rejecting the blessings I tried to give her. I know the struggle to understand and reason with a child who says, "I have it all under control." I have been there and still struggle. Since these motives are our default, we mistake them for our godly parenting principles. We say things like,

- "I'm the mature one here. I know best."
- "I've seen what happens when kids follow their dreams. Better stay close to home."
- "My parents were Christian parents and this worked for them. It will work for us too."

But since we are (hopefully) mature, godly parents, we must honestly look at our motives and do what is best for our kids, even though it will cause us discomfort and pain.

The father of the prodigal son didn't care what others thought when he gave the young man half of what he owned. Can you imagine giving one of your kids his share of your estate right now—knowing he would not spend it wisely? As I mentioned in chapter 1, Katie wanted some of her precious college money to rent an apartment. No, this wasn't half of our estate, but it was money we saved to help her with college. To us college is a big deal. It's what she needed to pursue her dream of being an artist. Why throw that dream away just to live a few miles from home?

Katie's Thoughts

I wasn't throwing my dream away. And if my parents had told me that was what they thought I was doing, I would have been really offended. I was only thinking about how to move my life forward. I was done living under my parents' roof. I think in the back of my head, I knew I could do it. At times I needed financial help and life advice. But I'm still alive! I did really well in school and landed a couple of jobs. I learned about relationship mistakes that I'm not sure I could have gone through at home. I wasn't thumbing my nose at my parents or disregarding their savings. I was showing my appreciation by making my own way in life. And honestly, what kid is actually 100 percent ready, financially or maturity-wise, to move out of her parents' house?

Your New Normal

Our stress is amplified when we try to look at our new situation through the old glasses. Our new situation—one in which our child is making decisions we don't agree with—requires a new paradigm. Our "normal life" is no longer what it once was. We have a different life—not the one we expected, but one that God knew was coming. If we are to be effective in it, enjoy it, and move ahead with our children, we must adjust our thinking. But that is the essence of life, isn't it? We never know what's coming next.

Here's a profound statement that will help you make sense of all this, and it's one I'm sure you'll want to underline—*it is what it is*. Powerful, I know. But it is packed full of the truth of your new reality. I can't tell you how many times I have said this to Gene regarding one of our girls' decisions—it is what it is. And now it's ours to live with.

Grieve the Life You Thought Would Be Yours

The first step is to mourn what we thought would be our reality for our family. Life isn't going to be the way we imagined it—at least not for a while. That is a hard pill to swallow. We will process this thought throughout our journey, but right now, will you start to accept this as your new normal and remember that God allowed it for your good and His glory?

Go ahead and grieve what won't be and what is now your new normal. It's okay. After Cynthia's daughter, Andrea, revealed to her she was a lesbian, one thing she grieved was the loss of a future son-in-law or grandchildren. "That was one of the most difficult things," Cynthia shared with me. I could hear the grief still in her heart.

God knows how you feel. He has grieved over His kids' decisions many times. The first time recorded in the Bible was right before the flood. In Genesis 6:5–6, we read that "the LORD saw that the wickedness of man was great on the earth, and that every intent of the thoughts of his heart was only evil continually. The LORD was sorry that He had made man on the earth, and He was grieved in His heart" (NASB).

God grieves for us in our bad choices. Judges 10:16 says, "And they put away the strange gods from among them, and served the LORD: and his soul was grieved for the misery of Israel" (KJV). It's inevitable that our kids will make decisions we don't agree with. Let yourself and your spouse grieve, and then move forward.

Find Someone to Walk with You

During this process it will be helpful to have someone to talk to who has been there and done it well. David's mom, Jan, advises parents to seek out safe people. She says, "You can't tell everyone everything." Pray for God to show you another parent or couple who has been on the same journey you are on. He will. James and Lisa have been on their journey with their son most of his thirty-seven years. They advise, "Have other couples you can unload with and pray with together. That kept us afloat."

Other friends who have been invaluable to me are my friends who have been on similar journeys as those of my girls. Some of the most profound comfort, reassurance, and support have come from friends who have walked similar paths as the ones my children are walking now. They also gave me the precious gift of loving, understanding, and not judging my daughters. They have been where my girls are and totally identify with them. They offered me encouragement without judgment.

As with most major life changes, your spouse may or may not be processing your child's decisions at the same pace you are. Donna and Bob differed in the way they approached Allison's choices. Donna was tempted to blame Bob because he wasn't parenting the way she thought was best. Now that they are through the hard years, Donna realizes, "Everything doesn't have to be resolved." Bob and Donna have a great marriage, but there are some issues they will never agree upon, and they've let them be. Just as with parenting, we choose our battles. During this time in your marriage, decide what's important to deal with and what's not. Give each other space to process in your own way.

Accept Your New and Different Life

As you move toward accepting your new reality, you realize life will no longer be the way you imagined it (and why do we think we are the ones to decide what a normal life looks like?). While it may not be the normal we expected, it is the normal God has for us. Your child's decision did not take God by surprise. He will work this for your child's good and His glory.

Accepting our new normal means we must reassess what's important in the big picture and decide what's not important. The first assessment for Gene and me was in regard to Katie's college money. It was important to us, but we weren't willing to lose or damage our relationship with Katie over a few thousand dollars. We saw that she was determined to live her plan with or without us, and since it wasn't a moral or legal issue, the college money became not as important as it once was.

Define What Is Important in Your New and Different Life

The decision about college money set the tone for all the other decisions about what's important in Katie's life and what's not. For me, this was when I started to erase some of the black-and-white lines I had drawn to define what I thought was the right way for her to live. These were my lines, not God's. We all have them. When our kids challenge them, we must acknowledge that we drew them, not God, and then we have to decide if we will let them come between us and our kids. Here are a few situations that challenge these lines:

- Choosing not going to college in favor of pursuing one's dream
- Taking a year off for a mission trip
- Pursuing full-time ministry instead of a secular career
- Having a child out of wedlock

After I spoke on this topic, a couple shared with me that their friends' son had fathered a child out of wedlock. The son, his girlfriend, and their new baby were making a home together. However, since they were not married, the parents did not invite the girlfriend or their new grandchild to Christmas. To that I can only say, *Really? That is how you want to start your grandparenting—by ostracizing your grandchild and his mother?*

Now is the time to decide what's really important. Let that guide you as you take up residence in your new and different life.

In our situation, this new and different life was not about us but about Katie living her plan. That was all she cared about. She did not care how we felt or what we thought was a good idea. If we had made it about us, we would have only put more distance between Katie and us. We would have become one more issue for her to deal with instead of becoming major players of influence in her life. I want to be the mom my kids call for encouragement, advice, and love. I don't want to be the mom they feel they must call as part of their adult-child duty while they endure my whining, chastising, and pity parties.

When Jan and George's son, David, started making decisions they didn't agree with, Jan learned she needed to change her perspective. She shed the things that didn't matter, including her perfectionism. Aren't our attempts at perfectionism a hypocritical facade to cover who we really are? We don't want others to know the real us or the realness of our families. Jan shared, "I had low self-esteem—I was such a people pleaser."

None of us is perfect. "For all have sinned and fall short of the glory of God" (Romans 3:23 NASB). If we are going to be fully engaged in helping our kids and building a relationship with them, we need to follow Jan's example—shed perfectionism and caring what others think—and dig in to what is truly important: helping our kids. When faced with a new situation or decision,

Jan's litmus test is, "How important is it? In two to three years is it really going to matter?"

There Are No Perfect Families

We struggle to adjust to our new paradigm because we are focused on other families that we think are perfect—perfect parents raising perfect kids. Whether these other families are perfect is not our concern. Comparing our kids, parenting styles, and situations to others only brings despair. We only see the surface. We have no idea of the reality of their relationships or their situations.

Deb's son, Brennan, followed his dad's example and abused alcohol and drugs. Through Brennan's high school and young adult years, Deb, now a single mom, tried to do what was best for her son. She cautions against playing the comparison game: "We compare ourselves to others, thinking other families are perfect." There are no perfect families. Even Jesus, though He was perfect, had an imperfect family (Mark 3:20–21; John 7:1–9). Comparing any part of our family situation to another family only hinders the process of becoming the parent your child needs.

Revisit Yourself as a Young Person

At this point, let's turn the focus from our children's decisions and instead focus on our own decisions. Think back to your past. What decisions did you make that your parents weren't happy with? These don't need to be bad decisions—just decisions that caused tension between you and your parents. Now add the decisions that were dumb, reckless, immoral, or illegal. This list is not to condemn you but to help you see life through your child's eyes.

One thing Gene did that was so helpful to Katie and me during this time was to operate out of his remembered perspective. For most of his growing-up years, Gene was raised by his great-aunt and uncle. They provided a stable, loving home for him and his twin brother. However, as we previously agreed, no family is perfect. As Gene and his brother grew to manhood and chose their paths, their uncle wanted control over Gene's decisions. He gave Gene the ultimatum either to cut his hair or to lose the promise of a substantial savings account. Gene, at that time an adult and a college student, refused to be controlled by the promise of money. He moved out the next day.

Gene's uncle gave him cause to move out. Maybe you have not done so with your child; however, your child's perceived reality is the same. Your child feels he must make his own decisions, and he doesn't see his decisions as poor.

Jan's son, David, recalls his thought process during his difficult journey. "Generally, I responded to my parents with hostility," he says. "I am still unsure why I was always this way around my family. Upon reflection, though, I have come up with a few theories. I felt safer blowing up on my family rather than [on] people who didn't love me because in the end, I knew my loved ones would forgive me. Also, I was just plain old defiant."

Nathan was raised in a loving Christian home. But Nathan

chose his own path, which took him on a long journey of drug and alcohol abuse. This led to unemployment and jail time. Looking back, Nathan states about his own decisions, "I consciously decided to rebel because I wanted to see how every evil thing felt. I wanted to know how drugs felt. I wanted to feel how an alcoholic felt."

Can you relate to any of these accounts?

- A need for independence
- A desire to be free from someone else's control (perceived or real)
- An urge to be defiant
- A curiosity about drugs or alcohol

Do you see any part of yourself or your siblings in your child? What are your thoughts about that?

Maybe you still need to forgive yourself (or others) for your past decisions. All of us have something in our pasts that we are not proud of. That's what Jesus came for—to wash away our pasts and to make us new and improved. Jesus lived on earth; was tortured, killed, buried, and resurrected; ascended into heaven; and is currently sitting at God's right hand—all to make us perfect and acceptable to God. If you're God's child, it's a done deal. God forgives your past. Now it's time for you to let it go and look forward to what God has for you. "Brethren, I do not count myself to have apprehended; but one thing I do, forgetting those things which are behind and reaching forward to those things which are ahead, I press toward the goal for the prize of the upward call of God in Christ Jesus" (Philippians 3:13–14).

The purpose of revisiting your past is not to make you feel

shame or demoralize you. The purpose is to help you remember from where you have come and to help you recognize all God has done for you. If He has worked so generously, lovingly, and mightily in your life, why do you think He doesn't delight to do so in your child's life? The Bible and all Christian history since is full of real people who made their own decisions and messed up big time. Yet God redeemed their lives, not only for eternity but during their time on earth. God is for us, and here's something you might have forgotten—He's for your kids too! Romans 8:31–32 (MSG) helps our perspective: "So, what do you think? With God on our side like this, how can we lose? If God didn't hesitate to put everything on the line for us, embracing our condition and exposing himself to the worst by sending his own Son, is there anything else he wouldn't gladly and freely do for us?" Our kids are part of the "us."

Now that the emotions and thoughts of your past are refreshed in your mind, use them (as Gene did) to understand what your child is thinking or going through. When Katie told Gene and me of her plan, Gene already knew it seemed foolish. Her words instantly transported him back to age nineteen: he was seated across from his uncle at the kitchen table, and his uncle slid a savings passbook to him and promised him the balance and more if he would only cut his hair.

This is your child's current reality. And it's your new normal. Based on truth or not, it's reality in your child's mind, and it's up to you how you will respond to their perceived reality. I know it doesn't seem fair. Everything in you wants to reason with your child however you can. But it won't matter. Not now, anyway. Your new normal is to wait a split-second before you respond. This is not the place to vent your emotions. This is the time for

you to set the tone for the next phase of life with your child—
unless, of course, you want to sit this one out. That would be a
gutsy move, because you have no guarantee he will circle back to
resume relationship with you after this season has passed.

I know this is not easy. I know it's not what you dreamed for
your child. But it is what it is. God has allowed it. Are you ready to
move forward to be the parent your child needs, build a lifelong
relationship with him, and show him the reality of God's love?

4

What in the World Am
I Doing Wrong?

Common Mistakes Parents Make

I don't know about you, but I've learned as much from watching people who aren't great examples as I have from those who are great examples. Sometimes the best way to learn what to do is first to learn what *not* to do. This chapter will show you what *not* to do as a parent when your kids make decisions you don't agree with.

As I said in chapter 3, we parents are often caught off-guard by our kids' decisions, so we are not ready with an appropriate response. Our first impulse may be to play the tape from our parents and respond how they did. As you have already discovered, this reaction most likely is not going to be helpful. Or maybe your reaction is to treat the circumstance like a hostage situation and give in to the demands of the alter ego holding your child prisoner. That doesn't work either.

What are you doing to put distance between you and your child?

The Servant Parent

The Servant Parent tries to woo the child back by anticipating and meeting her child's every whim. This parent feels if she can show her child how much she loves her by serving her then her child will turn from her poor decisions and come back. I observe this in many parent/child relationships. The parent knows the child is distancing herself, so the parent tries to appease the child by anticipating her every want.

Katie's Thoughts

Giving your kids or young adults everything they want teaches them that they don't need to do anything to participate in a relationship with their parents or anyone else. Their communication skills are injured because their parents don't demand anything from them. It's a pretty simple equation. You are training your kids that they can get the same reward from a healthy relationship without doing any of the work. And not only does that affect the parent/child relationship, but kids take those expectations into jobs, school, and so on. Of course, kids realize that their parents love them and are trying to show that love, but they also see that their parents are desperate and obviously lacking the courage or confidence to parent correctly.

Lindsay, one of my friends from school, had parents like that. She never saved any money because her needs were taken care of completely. She didn't worry about taking care of her vehicles because they would be replaced without hesitation.

Even when Lindsay was in her midtwenties, her mother continued to buy her groceries, make her appointments, and pay her
college loans. Lindsay never asked for any of these things, but
they were constantly given to her. This anticipation of a child's
needs and wants cuts out the parent-child communication and
respect. Lindsay's lack of relational skills was evident in her
friendship with me and her relationship with her boyfriend.
She seemed emotionally stunted in that she couldn't get past
shallow conversation with either of us.

There can be a healthy way to give to your children without enabling them. Your kids cannot mature emotionally when
they are still being treated like babies. Don't confuse this
behavior with affection. Being a Servant Parent is like being
a jailer. You are depriving your kids of necessary life skills that
will be difficult for them to learn elsewhere.

Parenting is not about power, but in our kids' eyes it can be.
What our kids view as power, we know is a respect issue. As parents our job is to teach our kids to respect us and God. We don't
give in to their wishes. We strive to be parents they can respect.
We don't lay down our God-given role of parent to make our
kids happy. Guess what—it won't. For the most part, our kids
have issues not because we aren't good enough parents. Our kids'
issues are heart issues. Yes, we play a part (and we'll talk more
about that), but our role will never be to cajole them into having
a relationship with us and making good decisions.

The Checked-Out Parent

The Checked-Out Parent is opposite of the Servant Parent.
The Checked-Out Parent gives up when it becomes evident

his child won't do as he wants. His reasoning may be, "I've done all I can. He doesn't listen to me anymore." The truth is, parents are still the most influential people in their children's lives.

The Checked-Out Parent can sometimes mistakenly believe that the church will do a better job of parenting his child. Tim, a youth pastor for sixteen years, and William, a youth pastor for seven years, agree that being a Checked-Out Parent is one of the major mistakes they see parents making. According to Tim, one of the most unhelpful things parents do regarding their teenagers is "not spending enough or quality time intentionally encouraging and discipling their teen." William says the most unhelpful parents are those who "spend no quality time with the child."

We naturally want to back off when our kids become distant and difficult, but this is the time we must move closer in their lives. William shares this insight: "Something else parents think they may be doing well, but is actually hurtful, is giving their kids too much space and freedom and in the process neglecting to disciple them and grow deep relationships with them." Our kids need to know we still love them no matter what. One way we show them that is by being involved in their lives, especially when their attitudes and actions are pushing us away. It's tough to balance giving children space to mature and grow into their own people while still nurturing a healthy relationship.

The Checked-Out Parent may be physically present but mentally checked in to his electronic devices. William shared with me about a teenage boy who tearfully confided in him that his family had no family time because his mom was always on the computer. Ouch. We hound our kids about too much texting or time on Facebook, but our actions speak more powerfully than our words ever will.

The sad truth parents miss is that their children want a loving, caring, involved parent. Our second daughter, Kelsey, is an elementary school teacher. She has taught in inner-city schools and middle-class schools. Even at the elementary-school level, she sees the kids' deep desire for relationship with their parents and the results when that doesn't happen. "One of my students said that his family ate dinner together but then everyone went their separate ways. He was left to play video games alone. One day he told me, 'I hate going home at night because I'm so bored.'

"My students were so hungry for attention that they would do whatever they needed to in order to get it. This meant getting in trouble, or performing below their actual reading level in order to get one-on-one attention with a teacher or aide. Children need to be cuddled, loved, and constantly reminded how special they are to their parents. I've seen what happens when students' lives are devoid of love, and it is heartbreaking."

The Gotcha! Parent

From the interviews of youth leaders and adult children who made decisions their parents didn't agree with, the one no-no that came up frequently is being a Gotcha! Parent. This parent keeps harping on sources of conflict. With the Gotcha! Parent, there is never a safe place in the parent-child relationship because the parent may bring up these issues at any time.

Parents become Gotcha! Parents by nagging:

- "When will you get a job?"
- "The deadline is coming to register for fall semester. Are you going to register?"
- "Are you getting up for church? We're leaving in thirty minutes."
- "Doesn't [fill in boyfriend's name] have a job yet?"

They bring up the source of disagreement every time they have a chance—especially when they're alone with their children.

- "I know you're tired of talking about this, but if you could just see my point of view . . ."
- "You know your dad is very worried about you, but he just can't express his emotions."
- "Do you really think this is a good idea? How do you see this turning out well?"

Probably the child's least favorite tactic of the Gotcha! Parent is the ambush—not to be confused with a legitimate intervention. In the ambush, the parent goes behind the child's back to enlist the help of the youth pastor or other influential people in the child's life. This seems like a good idea to the parent, especially when she doesn't know what to do next. But the leaders and kids I talked with all listed this in the "not to do" list. I'm not ruling out the importance of godly adults in our kids' lives. But when our kids are making decisions we don't agree with, a surprise talk from the youth pastor only serves to "build distrust [of] the mom and pastor [by the child]," states Keith, who's been in youth ministry for nine years. He adds, "I will do it, if the kid agrees." As parents we have more influence than we realize. We need only to use our influence effectively.

Katie's Thoughts

It's a vicious cycle: the kids won't tell their parents anything new because the parents will just use it to nag them about it later—and the parents don't know what to ask their kids about because they won't tell them anything new.

I highly doubt that kids will change their behavior based on constant nagging. The only thing that changed my behavior was maturing and eventually letting some of my parents' advice sink in. When my parents were disappointed in me, that's when I tried to figure out how my behavior was negatively affecting me—not because Mom constantly asked me about something we both knew wasn't going well in my life.

The Passive-Aggressive Parent

Passive-Aggressive Parents don't deal with their children's decisions in an honest and direct way. They may act calm or unaffected, but their emotions are churning. One way Passive-Aggressive Parents express their feelings is by taking out their emotions on someone other than the child. Katie talks about what she observed while visiting in a friend's home.

Katie's Thoughts

Talking about your kids in the other room so they can hear you, but not actually saying anything directly to them, is about as effective as buying them lunch every day so they will love you more. If you don't have the guts to talk to your kids about their decisions, then don't talk to anyone else about it in hearing range.

When I was a teenager, there was no way I would change my behavior just because I heard my mom complaining about it to my dad. In fact I think that drove my mom and me apart a bit. I found it hurtful that my mom wouldn't want to talk to me about an issue, even if it would end in an argument. That communicates that our relationship isn't strong enough or important enough for a fight. If my parents wouldn't try to communicate with me, then I was learning only how to not communicate with them and other people.

While visiting a friend I observed that his dad didn't want to talk to him, so he yelled at his wife because he was unhappy with their son's decisions. Well, that does a ton of good. Now not only was the son making decisions his father didn't agree with, but he has learned to avoid family confrontation and sees that it's okay to redirect anger at your significant other.

Honestly, the choice is between communication or passive-aggression. There is no in-between, and your kids, at any age, can tell the difference.

Another way to deal with repressed emotions is to divert those emotions to other less sensitive issues. This behavior is also called making mountains out of molehills. It confuses children because they know their parents are overreacting. The important issues are never appropriately addressed.

Katie's Thoughts

Hannah's parents always seemed to focus on the small things rather than the big picture. When Hannah was in high school, instead of giving her strict curfews or checking out the parties she went to, her parents yelled at her for not taking out the garbage or cleaning her room. At sixteen Hannah needed a different kind of parenting than when she was in junior high. But her parents weren't there for her. They didn't try to talk to her about the kinds of boys she was hanging out with in high school. So when she went to college she still chose boyfriends who were a bad influence.

I remember Katie sharing these situations with me when the girls were in high school. They wondered why Hannah's parents made such a big deal about her not doing her chores. Hannah's parents were scared to delve into the deep, important issues with their daughter; instead they picked fights over insignificant issues such as taking out the trash.

The Scared Parent

I believe most parents are scared because they feel that one wrong move on their part will cause their children to rebel (hello—that ship is sailing!) or bolt, and they'll never see them again. Except in extreme cases, this is a lie straight from, well, you know where. Deep down our kids love us and want us to show them love.

Katie's Thoughts

I know plenty of kids who never want to see their parents again. Their parents are making worse decisions than the kids are, and this affects them and their siblings. A coworker of mine was living with her mom and stepsister. Her mother was an alcoholic and was dating an alcoholic who lived with them as well. Eventually the situation became unsafe for my coworker and her stepsister. She had to take another job to be able to move out. After getting an apartment, she vowed never to go back home.

Kids know if their parents selflessly love them. They are keenly discerning and know if their parents care more about themselves than their kids.

As David, Jan and George's son, said previously, "I knew my loved ones would forgive me."

The Scared Parent is frustrated with his child's decisions and knows he can't continue to not act, but he is too scared to address the issue himself. So he tries to find someone else to deal with his child.

William, a youth pastor, agreed that this is a common mistake parents make: "Instead of having legitimate conversations with their kids, they come to the leaders to have them do the parents' job." I can relate. So many times I was convinced I was not the right parent for Katie. I never seemed to make progress or helped to guide her in making better choices. What I wouldn't have given for a mentor or youth leader or counselor to help her with her issues. Having other trusted, godly adults invested in our child would have been great, but Gene and I learned that through it all we were the most effective voices in Katie's life.

Tim also makes the point that "[parents are] not asking the tough questions because they are afraid of the answer. They're avoiding those conversations." Hannah's parents most likely did not want to hear the answer to questions like, "Who were you with? Where were you this evening? Was a parent home?"

Parents fear the answers to these questions. This fear inhibits discussion about more delicate issues like the child's sexual activity or possible drug or alcohol use.

The Compare-and-Despair Parent

A damaging response to your child's decisions is to compare her to a sibling, friend, or anyone doing what the parent finds acceptable. Who likes to be compared to anyone? The comparison game places the child's weaknesses against the other person's strengths. It's not fair. Nor is it the truth. Everyone has weaknesses and everyone has strengths.

Grace, now in her early thirties, made many decisions her parents did not agree with when she was in her early twenties. One of those decisions was to live with her boyfriend. Her mom tried to talk to her about their relationship and directly asked her, "Are you sexually active?" Grace's response was, "I'm not going to answer that." Grace's dad tried the opposite angle. He took the boyfriend out for breakfast. That did not go well.

Finally, before it was time for her parents to fly back home, they took one more shot. They came together for what Grace labeled "an ugly discussion with my parents."

Her parents played the comparison card. "Your siblings are living up to their potential, but you're not," they told her. That was it for Grace. She asked them to leave. They did, and Grace did not speak to her parents for six months. Granted, there were many factors in play here, but the final straw was the comparison her to her siblings. What did they think it would accomplish?

Think about it. What is the issue you're battling right now (finances, weight, strained marriage, job loss, etc.)? What if someone close to you said, "Your friends have plenty of savings, retirement, and money for their kids' college. Why doesn't your bank account show more for all your years of earning?" Or if your husband said to you, "Your sister looks great since she lost twenty pounds. Why don't you try to drop a few?" I don't feel especially inspired by any of these challenges, which compare someone else's strength to my weakness. In fact, these comments cause me to feel bad about myself and not very affectionate toward the person who said them to me.

Comparisons to siblings proved almost fatal for one family. Genesis 37:3–4 gives us the back story: "Now Israel loved Joseph more than all his children, because he was the son of his old age. Also he made him a tunic of many colors. But when his brothers saw that their father loved him more than all his brothers, they hated him and could not speak peaceably to him." No, the word "comparison" is not used in this passage, but the tone of theses verses is dripping with it. Can't you just hear Jacob (later named Israel) saying to his other sons—"Isn't Joseph so special? Doesn't the tunic look handsome on him?" If we back up to verse 2 we see that Joseph tattled on his brothers to Jacob: "This is the history of Jacob. Joseph, being seventeen years old, was feeding the flock with his brothers. And the lad was with the sons of Bilhah and the sons of Zilpah, his father's wives; and Joseph brought a bad report of them to his father." Ah, fertile ground for comparing good Joseph with the bad brothers: "Joseph tells me you boys have not been careful with the flocks and you spend more time throwing rocks at birds than doing your work. Why can't you be more conscientious like Joseph?"

Nothing breeds sibling rivalry like comparing one kid to another. The brothers consistently made decisions their dad didn't agree with. This comparison only made the situation worse. Later in chapter 37 Jacob sent Joseph once again to check up on his brothers. But the brothers were fed up with Joseph. Verse 18 says, "Now when they saw him afar off, even before he came near them, they conspired against him to kill him." The oldest brother, Reuben, saved him, only for Joseph later to be sold into slavery.

Jacob's comparison of Joseph to his brothers did not help any of his children. I know we can be exasperated with our kids, but comparing and despairing only makes the situation worse.

The Controlling Parent

The Controlling Parent is bent on fixing her kid. This parent's response is to rein in her child by controlling every area of her child's life. As I shared in chapter 1, when Cynthia's daughter Andrea announced her decision to pursue a lesbian lifestyle, Cynthia's first reaction was to pack up her daughter and bring her home. Cynthia's gut reaction told her that if Andrea was safe and sound at home, all would be well. Of course, Andrea would not go with her mom. She stayed put and pursued her gay lifestyle. Cynthia could not fix Andrea's heart issue.

In parenting there is no formula for a guaranteed result. Effective parenting takes selfless perseverance. We must know our kids and adjust our parenting styles according to what works for the individual child. What works for one child will not work for the next one (something you've learned if you've potty-trained more than one toddler). Presence versus control will look different in each child's life based on his age and situation. It goes back to the old but true cliché—pick your battles wisely.

The most challenging child may be the one who needs the most space. As I'm sure it is with your kids, my kids have very different personalities, and that calls for different parenting styles with each one. One personality is not better than the other; they're just different. For example, our youngest, Kerry, is a senior in high school, and her biggest "issue" (if it can be called that) is forgetting her personal and household chores. It sounds like a small thing, but personal responsibility is hugely important in becoming a mature adult. God expects us to be personally responsible: "For each one shall bear his own load" (Galatians 6:5).

Conversely, when Katie was a senior in high school, the personal responsibility issue took second place (or third or fourth) to the other situations we dealt with on a daily basis. Almost every day Katie left for school in a huff because we had fought. Katie made an issue out of everything I asked of her. Household chores were as much of a struggle as more important issues, such as who she was hanging out with. I, too, made a big deal out of everything. With Katie the personal responsibility issue could not be the battle we chose to fight with her. There were too many other safety and moral issues to deal with.

Katie's Thoughts

Every time I wanted to do something social, there was a fight. When I was in high school, my parents' rules were very strict. I was not allowed to do more than two social activities per week. Even then, when I left the house, my mom would be upset with what time I wanted to be home or where I was going. My mom didn't understand that I wanted a social life, and I didn't understand why she was trying to keep me from having one.

I tried to control the situation in order to bring Katie back to the happy, fun girl I knew was still in her but was being suffocated by her bad attitude. The boys she hung out with encouraged her disrespect and bad choices. I thought that if only I could get her away from them, she would change. But trying to control her life was not the way to bring about change.

The You're-Ruining-My-Life Parent

Our kids' ongoing decisions we don't agree with and the accompanying consequences often affect us like the aftershocks of an earthquake. We feel the effects when least expected and throughout all areas of our lives. When crisis strikes, our challenge is to not make life about ourselves.

Grace had a friend who also made decisions her parents didn't agree with. Her father was an elder in his church and experienced pressure. The church wasn't gracious and understanding of Grace's friend's lifestyle. The father wrote a letter to his daughter and let her know how *her* "sin" was affecting *his* life. The letter did nothing to help the relationship. The message the daughter heard from her father was, *It's all about me!*

Unfortunately, people will always feel they have the right to speak into your personal life. But this is not a reason to add another block to the wall between you and your child. We will talk more about this idea in chapter 9. For now remember, Mom and Dad, this situation is not about you. This is about your child's confidence in your love for her no matter what. Your goal is to nurture your relationship with her and keep the way back to the Lord obstacle free.

The My-Way-or-the-Highway Parent

The My-Way-or-the-Highway Parent is self-explanatory. This parent knows best. There are only two ways to look at life—the parent's way and the wrong way. Notice that this doesn't leave much room for exchange of ideas or the Word of God (I'm assuming these parents think God agrees with them on everything). I realize the stakes are high in parenting our kids, and Christian parents especially know this. But this vein of thought often produces a black-and-white mentality to everything in life. We spiritualize everything. There is right music and wrong music; there is right literature and wrong literature. There is a right way to dress and a wrong way to dress. My-Way-or-the-Highway Parents believe their way is the only right way, and all other ideas are wrong.

To avoid becoming this type of parent, we need to read through the Bible (yes, the whole Bible) and see for ourselves what God says is black and white. God leaves spacious room for us to express ourselves as He designed us. It is well within His boundaries of right and wrong.

The pick-your-battle mentality applies here well. Remember yourself as a young person. Were some of your ideas and beliefs not the same as your parents? Was the message from your parents that you were wrong about everything with which your parents didn't agree? Why do we expect anything else from our kids?

Nathan makes the point that even though he knew his parents loved him and loved God, he needed space. "I think they could have been a little less opinionated about my choices than they were," he says. "By that I mean that they could have just let me be a little more me. Then they might not have seen me rebel so much. If my choices were more mine, then I would have not strayed so far from their good choices."

I was the My-Way-or-the-Highway Parent—all the while believing I was doing what was best for Katie. I did not leave room for Katie to be the person God created her to be.

Katie's Thoughts

Something that I have been discussing with my parents is that we have different definitions of morality and foolishness. Everyone has a different way of looking at things and reacting to situations. So if you, a parent, are convinced that a decision is wrong and you can't understand why your kid is ignoring you, she probably isn't. She might not agree that it is wrong. That's why communication is key. If you talked to your child about which aspects you found unsettling and she tried to explain it to you, you might not see eye to eye, but at least there was an attempt. And after that conversation you can move on. Don't make more attempts to change her mind, which communicates that you don't trust her and you don't value her opinions. That's just another way to drive her away.

Unfortunately the My-Way-Or-The-Highway Parent is all too common, even if kids are not making poor choices. I know. I am a recovering one. I have also observed parents who make major issues out of nonissues—the child who runs a few minutes late in the morning, the occasional slipup in manners, clothes that are modest and appropriate but the parent declares reveal too much. The list goes on. Parents, we want to do a good job, but we must guard against provoking our children to anger (Ephesians 6:4). If you are the parent who can never be pleased, trust me, your child will stop trying. She will decide her own moral compass, and it will be a few degrees off from yours. I have experienced this and seen it in other families as well.

Hey, Mom and Dad, I know this has been a heavy chapter. You may be feeling like you can't or haven't done anything right. That wasn't the intent. I want to give you insight into your child's perceptions. I'm definitely not saying the kids are all right and we're all wrong. But in order to be effective parents, we need to know how our kids think and process. It's not about us, but we have a major part to play. Remember, we're all on a journey—so hang in there!

5

What Is Yours and What Is Not

The Truth About Parental Guilt and the Enemy's Lies

P arental guilt—there's nothing quite as heavy, demoralizing, and hard to unload. The feeling that you, the parent, have potentially messed up your kid is difficult to free yourself of.

As I stated earlier, Katie's junior high and high school years were hard for all of us. One day while having lunch with a coworker, I shared a little of my frustration in parenting Katie. I wasn't on a rant; it was more of the you're-not-gonna-believe-what-she-did-and-how-do-I-respond? conversation. My coworker launched into a lecture that seemed to last for eternity. Always maintaining a smile, she compared me to her parents, who, according to her, crippled her maturity, communicated with her poorly, and made her feel less than a priority to them. She went on to warn me (with a smile, don't forget) that if I continued my parenting style, my relationship with Katie would be doomed and Katie would be damaged for life. Her monologue was her emotional purge, and I was her emotional toxic dump site. Without a struggle, I accepted the guilt and lies about my parenting as she transferred her parents' issues to me.

I sat paralyzed, unable to speak. Up until this time I had never known my coworker to be anything less than kind. I couldn't believe she was saying those unkind words and placing a heavy load of despair on me. I wanted to make her stop but feared if I opened my mouth I would scream. Finally, she wrapped up her closing argument against me—still smiling—and I scraped up enough emotional strength to end our time and walk to my car. There I let the pain flow.

Wow. Was I really that bad of a mom? Was I dooming Katie to a life of poor self-esteem that she would always struggle to overcome? I couldn't shake the fear that my coworker was right, that I had no clue to the damage I was doing to my daughter. Throughout the day her words continued to burn deeper into my heart.

That evening I talked with Gene about the conversation. Gene is my biggest source of comfort but never at the expense of the truth. He said my coworker couldn't be more wrong and that this was more about her and her parents than me and my parenting. Still, I couldn't shake the guilt, the heaviness of heart, and the fear that I was permanently harming my daughter. A lie began to weave its way through my thinking. The lie: I was the reason for Katie's poor choices and our rocky relationship.

No parent is perfect. Our challenge is to sort out what our part has been in our children's decisions and consider our contribution to the rocky relationship. Then we can more clearly see what our children are responsible for.

The Parents' Part in the Fray

How have your words, attitudes, and actions contributed to your child's poor decisions or your difficult relationship? I confess that throughout my parenting career I've been almost all of the kinds of parents we discussed in chapter 4—some more than others. So my part in the fray has been multifaceted. As all our daughters have grown, I have made many different errors (and who hasn't?), depending on the situation and my level of maturity at the time.

Don't let the list of your parenting flaws from the previous chapter burn deep in your heart, like I did when my coworker unloaded on me. Honestly acknowledge your mistakes and prepare to move on. Soak in these wise words of Oswald Chambers: "Let the past sleep, but let it sleep on the bosom of Christ, and go out into the irresistible future with Him. Never let the sense of failure corrupt your new action."[1]

Understand that every parent is different and subjectively assesses their parenting style. Some parents are softhearted and take responsibility for any friction in the relationship or poor decisions by the child. Other parents believe they are God's infallible word to their kids, so any problems in the relationship or in their children's lives is the child's fault. Both extremes are dangerous.

To the parent who believes you are always right—you're not. There was only one person who was always right, and currently

He sits at God's right hand. You are God's precious child, and you are in process just as your child is in process. No one is the perfect parent. Humbly sit at God's feet and allow Him to gently show you the missteps, misunderstandings, fallacies, delusions, and misbeliefs you have lived by. Only then can you start to build a relationship with your children, whether or not they ever see life your way.

To the parent who believes your kid's situation is all your fault—it's not. Everyone has choices to make—including our kids. Take a minute now and give your child to God. Below is a little prayer to help you express your thoughts, if you like:

> *God, thank You for Your love for me and for my precious child. I know You love her more than I can. I'm choosing to trust You with her—her life, her decisions, her thoughts. Please keep her while she's living in what seems to me to be the distant land. Help her to become the person you planned for her to be. Hold on to her mama (or papa) while she's on this journey. I love You, Lord.*

Your child is an independent person from you, and God has a unique plan for his life. Part of that plan includes your child making his own decisions. God is more active in your child's life than you realize, and you need to separate yourself from him so you can see God's hand in his life. We may not have made it easy for our children to make the right choices, but we're about to change that.

This is the last part of our self-examination before we move forward, so let's make it count. Barring the extreme neglect of your child (if you did, please seek a professional Christian counselor's help), honestly list your negative contribution to the relationship. I'll start a possible list for you:

- Using phrases such as "you always," "you never," "why can't you . . . ?"
- Finding fault in your child more often than finding the positive—and telling your child so
- Not giving time and attention to really listen to your child; not being present and available
- Preferring one child over another
- Treating or speaking to your child disrespectfully

One of my biggest faults was taking everything Katie said personally. Her statements were directed at me, after all, so why shouldn't I take them personally? Here's why: because all this muck was way more about her than me. I was her safe person. When you think about it, the uglier she was to me, the louder she cried to me, *I love you and trust you won't desert me!* This is not to excuse her actions but to help us get our minds around the hurt and frustration our kids are experiencing.

The Child's Part in the Fray

Our kids are responsible for their words and actions, just as we are responsible for ours. They believe they are until we tell them they are not. When we make excuses for their poor behavior, fits, disrespect, and disobedience, we are telling them, *I know you can't help yourself, so it's okay to behave like this.* Ever since Katie was a child, she would become angry when she was given twice the consequences. I would always tell her, "You are being disciplined for your disobedience and then for your bad attitude toward your discipline." Most of the time Katie responded with anger or disrespect when given consequences for her actions. This response was her choice.

By now your child has learned which of your buttons to push to achieve her desired result. She knows when you will give in and how to manipulate you to do so. Consider the following list of behaviors your child might engage in that negatively contribute to the relationship. These are inexcusable behaviors, no matter how poorly you behave.

- Disobeying house rules, school rules, the law
- Hurling words meant to cut through your heart
- Not communicating with you
- Neglecting personal responsibilities—schoolwork, job, chores, and so on

The Truth About the Parent's Responsibilities

I believed the lie that if only I were a better parent, Katie (and our relationship with her) would thrive. After all, I was the one she butted heads with most often. I was the one who talked to her about her unkindness to her sisters and her disrespectful words and actions. I must be most of the problem.

Off and on I sensed God telling me this was not true, but I dared not trust that notion. Life was difficult with Katie because I made it that way. If it wasn't my fault, whose fault was it? Gene didn't clash with her like I did. Her sisters certainly didn't contribute enough in Katie's life to make her this miserable. No, the only person who could be blamed was me, her mother. I believed this lie until Katie was about nineteen or twenty.

God finally made it clear to me how wrong I was. We had had a few tough days with Katie and Gene and I were discussing the current issue. Normally I would have defaulted into *this-is-all-my-fault* thinking. But on this particular day it was as if God said to me, *This is the day you will believe My truth. Katie is making these decisions. You are not the cause.* What a revelation! I was not ruining my daughter's life! What a comfort to my aching mother's heart. It also removed a heavy load from my back. I was not the cause of Katie's bumpy life. Yes, she hurt from her past and, yes, as you have already seen, I did plenty to contribute to my share of the fray. However, Katie was the one responsible for her words and decisions, not me. Now I could proceed as a healthy mom (instead of one crippled by guilt) to repair our relationship and help my daughter navigate her life.

Deb, Brennan's mom, also struggled with guilt over her son's choices and let God bring her to the same conclusion: "We can't take the guilt. [I] can't blame anyone. My son made these choices."

I confessed my part in the fray to Katie. God began to show me what I did to trigger Katie's temper. (At times God used Gene to enlighten me!) Then I had a choice—would I change the way I communicated with my daughter, which required extra care for word choice and tone, in order to rebuild my relationship with her? Or would I remain the same and in essence say, *This is her problem. I am who I am. I've done nothing wrong?* I chose to allow God to change me. I'll talk more about this decision in chapter 7.

As God prompted me, I continued to apologize to Katie for my poor behavior. This is an ongoing part of keeping our relationship healthy. A couple of weeks ago, Katie and I sat down to the computer to work on this book. She said, "Mom, before we start, there's something I want to talk to you about."

She kindly and with tears explained to me how something I was doing was hurting her. She was right, and I told her so. I asked her forgiveness and told her I would do my best to improve. She accepted my apology and we grew closer from the experience.

Just as importantly, I owned my errors before God and purposed in my heart to respond better when those situations arose again.

James and Greg began "colliding" when Greg was in junior high. Their conflicts continued through Greg's young adult years. James's anger toward Greg's disobedience resulted in verbal and physical abuse. James has since owned his part to Greg and apologized. Greg has forgiven him. A sign of their healing relationship is the ritual of a certain handshake when they greet each other.

Cynthia and Frank also realized the part they played in their rough relationship with their daughter, Andrea. Cynthia shares, "She blamed both of us—particularly she lays a lot on her dad. In a counseling session with a pastor—all three of us—we apologized to her. She received it well and thanked her dad."

Our kids so often hear the message that they have messed up. Our confession of our part in the fray means the world to them. If you do only one thing I suggest in this book, ask your kids' forgiveness for your role in the conflict. Doing so tells them you care about them, want a real relationship with them, and love them no matter what.

The Child's Responsibility in the Fray

In our culture, personal responsibility is excused because what used to be considered a sin is now labeled an illness, a lifestyle choice, or a trait inherited from our parents. But God still holds each person responsible for his decisions; thus the need for a Savior. In his book *Systematic Theology,* Wayne Grudem states, "God has made us *responsible* for our actions, which have *real and eternally significant results.*"[2] He goes on to make the point that we cannot blame others for our actions: "Significantly, Adam began to make excuses for the very first sin in terms that sounded suspiciously like this: 'The woman whom you gave to be with me, she gave me the fruit of the tree, and I ate' (Genesis 3:12 RSV)."[3] Our kids have choices, and they make their own decisions.

Katie's Thoughts

I made the decisions I made for a number of reasons:

1. I thought they were the right decisions for me at the time.
2. I am stubborn, and I know what I want.
3. I didn't know what other decision to make. I didn't want to ask for advice because I thought I knew what the other option would be. I didn't know who to ask for a good in-between option.

Sometimes I knowingly made poor decisions to self-sabotage. I knew there would be a bad consequence, and I thought I deserved it for the poor decisions I made earlier. That's the problem with being able to think two and three steps ahead of yourself but still being too strong-willed to change your behavior. I honestly think it has to do with low self-esteem and habits of self-sabotage. I believed that I didn't deserve good successful outcomes, so I purposefully avoided them and created harder, messier situations for myself that ended in more work and pain.

This cycle continued because, after dealing with bad consequences for so long, I become used to it. I thought it was the only way to deal with situations. So it becomes a lifestyle—make poor decisions and deal with the consequences. Some people don't know how to succeed because they have taught themselves to avoid success.

Does Katie's explanation of how she used to make decisions help you understand that your child also processes his decisions? He is responsible for his choices.

Among our children's ongoing responsibilities is to follow house rules. Please, parents, make these reasonable. Most kids (and adults) cannot keep their living spaces spotless all the time, and we all forget to take out the trash occasionally. But within reason and godly grace, establish your house rules and how the members of the family are expected to fulfill them.

James and Lisa set behavioral standards for James and told him specifically what they expected. He agreed to comply, but when he disobeyed, they would renegotiate. Lisa summarizes, "He knew how to work the system."

We, too, set specific rules for Katie, because in her mind, if there wasn't a rule about it, it must be permissible. Instant messaging on the computer was the popular way of communication among teens when Katie was in high school. Reluctantly Gene and I allowed her twenty minutes of instant messaging per day. Since we didn't specify it must be during normal waking hours, she got up after we went to bed to instant-message with a boy we did not allow her to hang out with. We discovered this when one day, as Gene was at work on the computer, the printer printed out a conversation between Katie and this boy. Busted! We had the proof. Her response: "You didn't say I couldn't IM at night." Like I said—she needed a rule for everything.

Another nonnegotiable responsibility for our kids is to speak respectfully to everyone. It is our responsibility as parents to model respect, to teach our kids how to be respectful, and then to enforce respectful behavior with the other family rules. In 1 Samuel 2:27–36 God speaks to Eli, the priest, through a "man of God" regarding the disrespect of his sons toward God and their positions as priests. God chastises Eli with, "Why do you kick at My sacrifice and My offering which I have commanded in My dwelling place, and honor your sons more than Me, to make yourselves fat with the best of all the offerings of Israel My people?" (v. 29). When we don't teach and require respect from our kids, God says we honor our kids more than we honor Him. Respect is serious business to God.

Consider: Does your life reflect a respectful tone? Or do you put down your boss, your pastor, your spouse, your kids, or your parents? If you have a tendency toward disrespect, your children have probably caught it. Add this behavior to your list of things to own and apologize for.

If you do speak respectfully to others, your children know what respect looks like. They may need you to point out this respectful behavior to them, and you should let them know that it is what will be expected from them, even when they're angry. In 1 Samuel 2:30–34 God tells Eli the consequences for not teaching and requiring respect from his sons. God does not make excuses for our kids' lack of respect—and neither should we.

Moving Forward

You can't fix or save your child, and it is not your responsibility to do so. This attitude goes back to the lies we believe as parents—if we were better parents, our kids would be strong Christians. What a fallacy! God is the perfect parent, but His kids are not perfect—just take a look in the mirror. Judas spent three years living with Jesus. He knew Him better than almost anyone in history. But he had a choice, and he chose to betray Christ. If anyone could have saved Judas, it was Jesus, but Jesus gave Judas the choice to accept Him or reject him. Judas chose rejection.

In Matthew 19:16–22 a rich young man comes to Jesus and asks, "Good Teacher, what good thing shall I do that I may have eternal life?" Jesus answers, "If you want to enter into life, keep the commandments." The young man says he's done that, so what's next? Jesus tells him, "If you want to be perfect, go, sell what you have and give to the poor, and you will have treasure in heaven; and come, follow Me." But the young man was wealthy and couldn't do what Jesus commanded him to do. Verse 22 says, "He went away sorrowful, for he had great possessions." Jesus let him walk. Jesus held out eternal life with Himself for the young man, but the young man chose his wealth—and Jesus let him.

We cannot persuade, fix, or save our children. In the next chapters we will talk about positive things we can do, but first we must realize what is *not* ours to do. Only God can bring about repentance.

The most powerful thing we can do for our kids is pray for them. Jesus tells us to how to pray in Matthew 7:7–11. He said, "Ask, and it will be given to you; seek, and you will find; knock, and it will be opened to you. For everyone who asks receives, and he who seeks finds, and to him who knocks it will be opened" (vv. 7–8). *Strong's Exhaustive Concordance* comments on the meanings of the words "ask" and "seek." "Ask," it says, "is strictly a demand of something due." "Seek," it says, "implies a search for something hidden."[4] Jesus tells us to "demand something due" and "search for something hidden." "Knock" means just that— knock. But Jesus tells us to make the effort—*Knock on My door. Demand what is due you. Search for the hidden answer you need.*

Jesus wants us to come and knock on His door, not to sit back and take whatever comes into our families' lives. He wants us to demand what is due. I am not saying to come to Jesus with an attitude of entitlement, but I believe it is our responsibility and privilege to demand that the enemy not have his way in our kids' lives and that our kids come to know Jesus as their Savior. This is God's will—God does not want any to perish "but that all should come to repentance" (2 Peter 3:9). When we pray in this way, we are boldly coming to God, not demanding our rights but asking Him to actively work in our kids for their good. It is our job as parents to be our children's advocates in prayer.

Jesus also wants us to search for the answers we and our kids need. Throughout Katie's teen years I was desperate for a word of inspiration or direction from someone who truly understood our situation. From time to time I found myself in conversation with moms or adult children whose journey was similar to ours. As they shared their stories (or even a sliver of their story), I grabbed onto one thing they said—maybe a word of hope or one thing that worked for them. As I collected these stories, I gradually wove them into my parenting repertoire and called on them often. Jesus has the answers we need, but we must ask for them and seek them out.

Luke also records this account of Jesus' teaching, but in Luke it comes after Jesus taught on persistence in prayer. Here He told the story of a man who goes to his friend's house at midnight and asks for food to feed a traveller who has come to visit. The friend said, "Do not trouble me; the door is now shut, and my children are with me in bed; I cannot rise and give to you" (Luke 11:7). But Jesus made the point that we must persist: "I say to you, though he will not rise and give to him because he is his friend, yet because of his persistence he will rise and give him as many as he needs" (v. 8). Jesus tells us to persist in prayer—in demanding what is due us, searching for the hidden answers we need, and knocking till we get an answer. Prayer is not a passive way to spend our time until we gain influence in our kids' lives. Prayer is the way we wield influence in our kids' lives.

I'm not pretending to understand how prayer works or how God answers our prayers. But one thing I know—God is trustworthy. I can and do trust Him. I haven't always been able to say that, not because God wasn't trustworthy at some point but because I didn't trust Him. Whenever a new difficult situation came into my life, I sensed God saying, *Will you trust Me?* I wanted to, but fear of "what if" gripped me. *God, what if I trust You and something worse happens?* Through each challenge I walked with God and obeyed as best as I knew how, all the while holding my breath and waiting for something worse to happen. But God took me through each situation, and I always ended up on the other side thinking, *Wow. God was faithful. It was hard, but He took us through it and worked for our good.*

This is exactly the point Jesus made as He finished this teaching on prayer in Matthew 7:11. He assures us that God will answer our prayers with "good things to those who ask Him!" *Good* is defined as "intrinsic benefit."[5] Just as your definition of good differs from your child's definition of good, so God's definition of good differs from ours. I define a good evening as one that includes a nice family dinner and time spent together watching a movie or playing a game, with everyone in bed by ten to get a good's night sleep. My twenty-three-year-old daughter, Kelsey, defines a good evening by going out with her boyfriend. Hm, no mention of Mom there—except maybe as Kelsey shuts the door behind her when she leaves the house. Our definitions of *good* are very different. (Of course, when I was twenty-three, my definition of good would have been exactly the same as Kelsey's!)

God tells us, too, that He defines *good* differently than we do: "'For My thoughts are not your thoughts, nor are your ways My ways,' says the LORD" (Isaiah 55:8). Implied here is that we cannot, nor will we ever, be able to really understand God's ways. This is where trust comes in. Jesus tells me it is my job to pray, and God will give good things to my family and me. Since Jesus doesn't give busy work, there must be value in my prayers. I think I'll trust Him on this and continue to knock on His door and do what only I can do for my girls—pray with their mother's heart.

Just a Minute...

The remaining chapters of the book will move us forward as we take positive steps toward healing our relationships with our children and do our part to clear the obstacles on their path to God. Before continuing to chapter 6, I encourage you to pause for a moment until you decide you're ready to move forward in a positive way.

Think through the issues we've discussed so far. In what areas are you having trouble agreeing with God that you need a heart for change or forgiveness? Go ahead and jot them down. Take whatever time you need to work through the Questions for Reflection and Discussion for chapters 1 through 5 (found at the end of the book)—maybe with a trusted friend or mentor. Ask God to give you wisdom and strength as you work through any issues that might be a barrier to your ongoing development as a healthy parent.

Then let's move into the rest of the book together to build on this foundation with positive, practical applications.

6

They Think You Are God (Not Really, but Pretty Close!)

Showing the Real God to Your Child

When did you first realize God's love for you? It wasn't until I was well into my adult years that I did," my friend Claudia Mitchell asked a group of women gathered in my home for our monthly mentoring evening. Claudia (coauthor of *One Girl Can Change the World* and director of women's ministries at Sherwood Oaks Christian Church in Bloomington, Indiana) voiced what most of us never want to admit to ourselves, even after years of Sunday school and church: we don't really know that God loves us.

I silently agreed with Claudia. I grew up singing "Jesus Loves Me," but I don't remember any sermons on the love of God. I remember plenty of sermons telling me to straighten up or else.

I'm not saying the pastor didn't talk about God's love, but it's the "fire and brimstone" preaching that stuck. Maybe your experience was similar. Or maybe you didn't grow up in the church and your image of God is put together like a jigsaw puzzle with pieces coming from various sources. As a result, your idea of God isn't accurate either.

First John 4:8 tells us, "God is love." The Bible is full of God's commands and instructions for life. God loves us and knows it is for our best when we love Him and obey His commands. God is just, and with His justice comes consequences and punishment for our sin. Wayne Grudem explains this aspect of God's character: "As a result of God's righteousness, it is necessary that he treat people according to what they deserve. Thus, it is necessary that God punish sin, for it does not deserve reward; it is wrong and deserves punishment."[1] Both God's love and His justice were shown when He gave His Son, Jesus, so we can be "justified freely by His grace through the redemption that is in Christ Jesus, whom God set forth as a propitiation by His blood, through faith, to demonstrate His righteousness, because in His forbearance God had passed over the sins that were previously committed, to demonstrate at the present time His righteousness, that He might be just and the justifier of the one who has faith in Jesus" (Romans 3:24–26).

God went to a lot of trouble to show His love and still satisfy His righteousness. How then did the church become so unbalanced in its presentation of God? Some churches lean heavily on God's love and try to push His justice in the storage closet, only to be brought out in severe situations. Other churches wield the heavy gavel of God's justice, while His love is tied up and gagged in the back room.

With countless inaccurate views of God, is it any wonder we are confused? As a result, we do not present an accurate view of God to our children. We absorbed flawed theology about God, and now we are passing it on to our kids.

Tim Kimmel, in his book *Grace-Based Parenting*, states, "They [parenting styles] are the result of a parent's theology. Their theology is a combination of the way they view God and the way they think He views them. If we have flawed theology regarding God's attitude toward us, it can automatically create a chain reaction of flawed decision in how we raise our children. It can also set up our children to miss the joy of God, the heart of God, and the power of God in their personal lives. This is a recipe for the child to rebel and reject a parent's primary belief system."[2] We reflect how we view God to our kids by how we parent our kids:

- How we show them love
- How we speak to them
- How we listen to them
- How we treat them when they mess up
- How (if) we celebrate their victories with them
- How (if) available we are to them
- How we forgive them
- How patient we are with them

What does our parenting teach our kids about God? The reason we want our kids to know we love them no matter what is not so we have someone to care for us when we are old. It is so our kids will know God, accept Christ, and then live the abundant life Jesus promised here and for eternity. Before we can show God to our kids, we must first have an accurate view of God ourselves.

We must consider how God treats us. God went to much trouble and gave His most precious and only Son to have a relationship with us.

How God Treats Us

For a closer look at God's character, let's unpack Psalm 103:8: "The LORD is compassionate and gracious, slow to anger and abounding in lovingkindness" (NASB).

God Is Compassionate

Compassion is sympathy moved to action. In Luke 10:25–37 Jesus tells the parable of the good Samaritan:

> "A certain man went down from Jerusalem to Jericho, and fell among thieves, who stripped him of his clothing, wounded him, and departed, leaving him half dead . . . But a certain Samaritan, as he journeyed, came where he was. And when he saw him, he *had compassion*. So he went to him and bandaged his wounds, pouring on oil and wine; and he set him on his own animal, brought him to an inn, and took care of him." (vv. 30, 33–34; emphasis added)

The Samaritan was overcome by his emotions for the injured man. He acted on his emotions and physically cared for him.

Compassion is also used in Luke 15 to describe the actions of father of the prodigal son: "And he arose and came to his father. But when he was still a great way off, his father saw him and *had compassion*, and ran and fell on his neck and kissed him" (v. 20; emphasis added). The father loved his son so much that when he saw him coming—looking rough and ragged—his emotions overtook him. He ran to meet him, hugged him, kissed him, and then threw a huge party for him. He gave his son what he didn't deserve—compassion.

God has compassion on us. "Just as a father has compassion on his children, so the LORD has compassion on those who fear Him" (Psalm 103:13 NASB). God gives us what we don't deserve. He forgives our past. He brings us into His family. He loves us so much that He cares for every detail of our lives. He helps heal our hurts and messes.

We show compassion to our kids by helping them without enabling or encouraging sinful behavior. As I said in chapter 1, when Katie said she was moving out, the Holy Spirit gave me the red alert that I needed the right response immediately. Either I was on board or I wasn't. Never being one to miss the action, I jumped on board. I went through the house and pulled out extra pans, dishes, and towels. Then I bought a bucket and filled it with cleaning supplies. I didn't agree with her decision, but I did what I could to help her.

God Is Gracious

Gracious means "to bend or stoop in kindness to an inferior; to favor."[3] There is no greater understatement than to say God is our superior. This gives us some idea of the degree to which God stoops to show us kindness and favor. God is gracious to us every minute of every day. He exemplified graciousness when He sent His Son Jesus to take on a human body and live with human limitations.

The father of the prodigal son graciously "divided his property between them" (Luke 15:12). He gave his younger son his portion of everything he owned. He stooped to show favor to his son.

Jan and George's son, David, shared one way his parents showed their love and grace: "They would take me on special trips and vacations." In the midst of the grief he brought to their lives, would anyone blame them for taking a trip alone to get away from it all? But Jan and George intentionally built a relationship with their son and included him in the fun. All those trips and vacations spoke love to his heart even when he didn't respond to their love.

God Is Slow to Anger

God is slow to anger. He does not have a short fuse. He is longsuffering. He is patient with us.

We don't know how long the prodigal son was in the distant country, but it was long enough to spend everything his father had given him. This might have taken a little while, given that there were no expensive sports cars, big-screen TVs, or electronics to gobble up his money like there are in today's economy. Enough time passed for a severe famine to take hold of the country and put the boy in dire straits. Finally, the boy was hired by a farmer and given the job of feeding the pigs. In all this time, we have no indication his father was seething in anger for his son's sin and poor decisions. In fact, the father was always on the lookout for his son. When he finally saw him, he felt compassion for him and ran to him.

I eventually lost my shell-shocked attitude. When Katie came to us with a certain tone in her voice that communicated *I'm going to say something you're not going to like*, I learned not to be upset. I listened (and still do) to what she said and then gave her the best advice I knew. I stuck with biblical principles, not beating her over the head with the Bible but speaking God's truth without the Christian lingo. I did not say "I told you so" or "If you wouldn't have (fill in the blank) this wouldn't have happened." We didn't try to shield her from her consequences but helped her make the best decision given her circumstances. No amount of anger would help her or the situation.

God Abounds in Loving-kindness

The *Ryrie Study Bible* makes this comment about God's loving-kindness: "It means loyal, steadfast, or faithful love and stresses the idea of a belonging together of those involved in the love relationship. Here [Hosea 2:19 NASB] it connotes God's faithful love for His unfaithful people."[4] God continually loves us even when we are unfaithful (which, if we are honest, is most of the time).

The father of the prodigal son kept faithfully loving his son, even though that son didn't show the slightest concern for his father. Notice the father let the son go to the distant country, where he "squandered his estate with loose living" (Luke 15:13 NASB). The father couldn't have been pleased with his son, but he never forgot that he was his son.

Take a deep breath. I hear you saying, *But I have loved him for a very long time!* I know. Brennan, now thirty-five, tested his mom's (Deb) love and patience. In high school he became friends with a boy who was, in Deb's words, "on the streets." This friend stirred up rebellion in Brennan. When he was a senior, Brennan was arrested for trying to sell marijuana at school. He was suspended, and his family had to move to a new school so he could graduate. His journey was a downward spiral of drinking, DUIs, drugs, and prison. Deb encourages parents, "We can love our kids and not like what they do." In the coming chapters we'll talk more about what that looks like. We show God to our kids by how we persevere in loving them.

God Is Patient with Us

Paul states in 1 Timothy 1:16: "But for that very reason I was shown mercy so that in me, the worst of sinners, Christ Jesus might display his immense patience as an example for those who would believe on him and receive eternal life" (NIV). Paul shares that he believed he was "the worst of sinners," and still God showed "immense patience with him" as an encouragement for the rest of us. If God was this patient with Paul, who persecuted the early church "to the death, binding and delivering into prisons both men and women" (Acts 22:4), He is this patient with us.

We don't know how long the son was in the distant country, but it must have been months or even years. If your child has been on a journey of making decisions you don't agree with, you know the agony of these months and years. The stress it puts on you and your family makes the passage of time painful. This makes the father's response to his son even more amazing. It wasn't as if the son spent only a few wild days in Vegas; the father was waiting expectantly for his son's return for a long time. He patiently waited for his son's repentance. What is missing in this story is just as powerful as what is said. There is no sign the father complained about or badmouthed his son. How could he and still have the compassion and love he shows for his son upon his return?

This is the patience we are called on to show to each other, including our kids. Wayne Grudem sheds light on how we can show God's patience: "As with most of the attributes of God that we are to imitate in our lives, patience requires a moment-by-moment trust in God to fulfill his promises and purposes in our lives at his chosen time. Our confidence that the Lord will soon fulfill his purposes for our good and his glory will enable us to be patient."[5] Our confidence is not only that God works all things for our good and His glory, but also that God will work all things for our children's good and God's glory. As Deb, Brennan's mom, says, "You just gotta hang in there with them." Note the prodigal son's father is not rolling in his child's mess with him. His anger doesn't burn hotter as time passes. He is on the homestead with a heart that says, *When you're ready to turn your life around, I'm here—and I'll even run to meet you!*

The scene in Luke 15:20 speaks richly in regard to parenting. The father was ready for his son to come home. He had worked through his hurts and was ready to reconcile. The father's arms were not crossed but open. In the same way, God is always ready for relationship with us. Jesus' work on the cross made this possible.

God Is Available

God is always available to us. By putting into practice all you're learning, you say to your child, "I'm here for you." Be available. Your kids *need* to know they are your priority—over work, over your selfish distractions. Yes, your marriage comes first, but some parents spend more time on each other (and their friends) than is needed while the kids are left to fend for themselves. Kids can sense when they are not a priority.

Church is important, but be careful. Church is not our relationship to God. An evening spent as a family or time spent taking your children out for a movie or coffee is worth more than what any youth group leader can pour into them. Availability to your kids shouts love to your kids. Be home when they're home. Be available to help when they need it. Be available to listen when they feel like talking.

I recently went back to college. I thought I would be invisible to the young students, and that would have been okay with me. Instead I was the "popular kid"—the one the other students wanted to talk to. I was amazed. I'm an old mom. Why would they talk to me? I shared my amazement with Katie. Her response: "Mom, they like you because you listen to them. Nobody listens to them and you do." That's heartbreaking.

Even when your kids give off the air of *Don't bother me,* they want someone to care. Recently we were at a get-together at our friends' home. Their fifteen-year-old daughter had a few of her friends over too. The kids hung out in the family room in the basement and the adults were in the living room on the main floor. I noticed that one cute girl followed my friend around and chatted with her nonstop. The girl was fresh-faced with a sweet personality. Later I was sad to learn that she had become sexually active following her dad's death. Her stepdad is not nice to her, and no one spends time with her. She finds the attention she craves with an upperclassman boy. Is this what we want for our kids?

Being available for your child means making sacrifices on your part. Be there when they come home from school—even when they're in high school and college. Have food. That especially speaks that you care. Take their calls and return their texts immediately. One way I keep in touch with Katie is taking time to talk to her when she calls. Katie doesn't call for a quick chat. When she calls, it's because she needs to verbally process whatever is going on and get advice or encouragement. If I can't talk right then, I let her know and tell her when I will have time. I make this time as soon as possible.

Being available for your kids shows them God is always

available to them. This reminds me—do your kids see you taking advantage of God's availability in prayer and Bible reading? We want our kids to come to God, but are we making the way or just pointing the way?

Nathan's parents, Susan and Gary, showed him the way. "My parents are very godly people. I knew from my youngest memory that my parents were happy and taken care of because they loved God. . . . God was good, and I knew that because of how He dealt with my parents." Through Nathan's years of rebellion, drugs, alcohol, and prison, the one thing he never forgot and knew in his heart was that his parents loved God, and God loved and cared for his parents. They cleared the path to God for their son by the way they lived out their relationship with God.

The Enemy's Lies

The enemy's most effective weapon to render Christians impotent is his masterful use of lies. Because he is the "father of lies" (John 8:44 NIV), no one does it quite as well as he does. The following lies keep you powerless to trust God, to build a healthy relationship with your child, or to show God to your child.

Lie #1: God Has Given Up on Your Child

Your child is not too great of a challenge for the love of God. In Luke 15, right before the story of the prodigal son, Jesus tells the parable of the lost sheep.

> "What man of you, having a hundred sheep, if he loses one of them, does not leave the ninety-nine in the wilderness, and

go after the one which is lost until he finds it? And when he has found it, he lays it on his shoulders, rejoicing. And when he comes home, he calls together his friends and neighbors, saying to them, 'Rejoice with me, for I have found my sheep which was lost!' I say to you that likewise there will be more joy in heaven over one sinner who repents than over ninety-nine just persons who need no repentance" (vv. 4–7).

God will pursue your lost sheep. God would love nothing more than to bring her back to the fold. Remember, God's loving-kindness and patience toward us is the same He has for our kids.

Lie #2: God Is Ashamed of Your Child, and You Should Be Too

God is no more ashamed of your child than He is ashamed of any of His children. In Luke 15:20, we read that when the father saw his son "still a great way off, his father . . . had compassion, and ran and fell on his neck and kissed him." That does not sound like a father who was ashamed of his child. If God is not ashamed of him, neither should we be. Our kids sense how we feel about them without us saying a word. If your words, tone of voice, actions, or attitude hint of shame, your child will know it and may transfer those thoughts to God as well. Why would a child want to have a relationship with her parents or with God if she feels they're ashamed of her?

Lie #3: God Will Never Bless or Restore Your Child After All He's Been Through

Maybe you believe this about yourself as well, but it's a lie. God will use us till our dying breaths if we'll cooperate with Him. Moses sinned greatly by not believing God and not honoring Him before

Israel, so he wasn't allowed to go into the promised land (Numbers 20). But he took the nation of Israel right up to it (Deuteronomy 34). Moses is honored throughout the Bible—he is called the most humble man ever (Numbers 12:3); he appeared at Jesus' transfiguration (Matthew 17:2); God said of him, "He *is* faithful in all My house. I speak with him face to face, even plainly, and not in dark sayings; and he sees the form of the LORD" (Numbers 12:7–8); and Jesus spoke highly of him throughout the Gospels.

For a New Testament example of blessing, restoration, and amazing ministry, my first thought always goes to Peter. Luke 22:54–62 relates the account of Peter denying Jesus three times before the cock crows: "Immediately, while he [Peter] was still speaking, the rooster crowed. And the Lord turned and looked at Peter" (vv. 60–61). Talk about failing Jesus. Here Peter is the one acting ashamed of His Lord, and then Jesus turns and looks right into his eyes. As far as we know, Peter doesn't see Jesus again until after His death and resurrection. In John 21:15–19 Jesus restores Peter to a place of leadership and ministry in His church.

No child is hopeless. God is waiting for your child to return to Him to bless him and use him.

Lie #4: You Are the Conduit of the Holy Spirit to Your Child

You are *not* the voice of God to your child.

We are not responsible for continually reminding our children of their mistakes, poor decisions, or sins. We are not responsible for offering a life-plan to our kids. Our kids know how we feel about their issues. They've heard us quote chapter and verse to them. Now is not the time to beat them up with the Scriptures, but to live what we believe. Sometimes the best thing we can do is let our children fail and keep our mouths shut.

Lie #5: Good Parents Ride the Roller Coaster with Their Kids

It is not your responsibility to ride the roller coaster your child calls his life. God doesn't ride roller coasters either. Your child's decisions may be one wild ride after another, but it's not your job to let those decisions define your life or your day. God loves us, but our poor choices do not derail God's plans. "I know that you can do all things; no purpose of yours can be thwarted," Job said to God (Job 42:2 UPDATED NIV).

Matthew 19:16–26 gives the account of the rich young ruler who asked Jesus what he must do to have eternal life. After a conversation with Jesus that ended with, "Go, sell what you have and give to the poor, and you will have treasure in heaven; and come, follow Me," the young man "went away sorrowful, for he had great possessions" (vv. 21, 22). Jesus let him go. Jesus resumed teaching His disciples. Yes, I'm sure Jesus was very sad, but He didn't let this young man's poor decision define His day or derail God's plan for His day.

You step off the roller coaster by refusing to be in turmoil when your child shares his latest mess. You refuse to step back on the roller coaster when you don't rush in to rescue him. Advise biblically, but don't step in to protect him. You are in his life as a steady, loving parent, not someone who makes excuses for his poor behavior.

This leads us to the next lie.

Lie #6: It's Our Job to Keep Our Kids Happy or Happy with Us

Your child may try to guilt you for his mess, but you didn't make it, so the guilt is his. The father in the parable stood his ground with his younger son by letting him have his "loose living," come to the end of himself, repent, and return home. The father also held his ground with his older son when the prodigal returned. Read a little further in the prodigal son story and see how the older son reacted when his pig-feeding brother came home to a hero's celebration:

> "But he was angry and would not go in. Therefore his father came out and pleaded with him. So he answered and said to his father, 'Lo, these many years I have been serving you; I never transgressed your commandment at any time; and yet you never gave me a young goat, that I might make merry with my friends. But as soon as this son of yours came, who has devoured your livelihood with harlots, you killed the fatted calf for him" (Luke 15:27–30).

The father did not cajole his younger son to stay but loved him when he returned. The father kindly spoke truth to the older son in hopes he would celebrate with everyone else (vv. 31–32). However, the text does not indicate that the brother changed his mind, and neither did the father. The father loved both sons and did not change his parenting to make either son happy with him.

God does not try to appease us so we'll make better choices. We show God to our kids by being a strong, steady parent, not a parent they can manipulate. Oswald Chambers calls us to "the strong calm sanity that Our Lord gives to those who are intimate with Him."[6]

When David wouldn't go back to college after Christmas break, Jan and George realized he needed help. His counselor suggested that they do an intervention in order to place him somewhere to get help. During the intervention Jan broke down and cried. She recalled, "The worst thing I did in front of my son was cry.

It stopped all communication and caused more guilt. It belittled me as the weaker person." When we exhibit strong, calm sanity, we show our kids we are worthy of respect and will love them no matter what.

Showing the real God to our kids is an endless job and one for which we'll never be adequate. However, it is our job because we are the parents. Let this calling keep you at the feet of God and in constant contact with Him. Show your kids the love God shows you. Be there for your kids—even if you don't know what to say, be there. The rest will come.

7

Oh, So That's How to Be a Cool Parent

Practical Ways to Build Lifelong Relationships with Your Kids

D o you know who pestered me the most to pursue writing this book after I'd been speaking on the material for three years? Do you know who was truly concerned about me when last winter God pulled me off to the side of the road for a few months with no writing opportunities and very little speaking ministry prospects? Who came to me on more than one occasion and said, "Mom, when are you going to work on your book?"

Katie. Yes, Katie, the one who inspired this book and who is still living life her way, is my number one encourager and exhorter to write this book. I'm amazed at the relationship we have. We are still two very different people. We both know the topics to steer around because we'll butt heads two sentences into the conversation. But we are each other's biggest cheerleaders.

How did that happen? On my part—lots of prayer, dying to self, and letting God change me. I'm not bragging in any fashion; I'm stating the facts. Any good that I pour into my girls has come from God. He changed the heart of this uptight, prideful, anger-issue mom. God worked in Katie's heart too. He helped her forgive me and see my heart of love for her all the while maturing her.

There is so much you, the parent, can do to build a relationship with your child. We will discuss building bridges to your child and then exercising healthy boundaries in those relationships. But first we must show our kids we mean business in building a relationship with them.

Establishing Ground Rules

Decide your bottom-line nonnegotiables. I mean *bottom-line*. I encourage you to use moral and legal guidelines. For Gene and me, our nonnegotiables are an extension of our house rules. Our kids know them. Below is a list to consider when determining your nonnegotiables:

- No illegal behavior.
- Drinking—will depend on your house rules. If you and your spouse drink, what are your guidelines? Will your child honor those or would it be better to not have alcohol in the house to avoid conflict?
- No sharing a bedroom with a person of opposite gender unless married.
- No off-color or swear words, including taking God's name in vain.

- Friends are welcome as long as they abide by the house rules too.
- No undermining parental authority with other siblings.

With your guidelines established, you are ready to build a healthy relationship with your child. As we'll discuss, there is much you can do to grow this relationship, but how far it grows depends on your child. Romans 12:18 says, "If it is possible, as much as depends on you, live peaceably with all men." Relationships work like a tandem bike—best when two people are pedaling together.

Building the Bridge

The bridge to your child might need many repairs, or you may have burned it to the ground and need to start from the ground up when rebuilding your relationship. Whatever degree of bridge building your relationship requires, the situation is not hopeless. Remember the words of Gabriel to Mary: "For with God nothing will be impossible" (Luke 1:37). As you build the bridge of relationship to your child, seek God's guidance and ask for His mighty working in your child, yourself, and your relationship. He is faithful, and nothing is impossible with God.

Don't Take the Bait

Our kids know how to push our buttons like no one else does, and we return the favor. The next time you communicate with your child, overlook the little things that bug you and that easily escalate into an argument. Katie's artistic personality means she is naturally messy. When she comes in the house for a weekend visit, she dumps everything just inside the door. Her large purse, computer case, at least one basket of laundry, and various art materials lay at the end of the breakfast bar in the busiest traffic area of the house. When I lightheartedly ask her to help me move her things, she does so eagerly. But a few years ago that would have caused a minor eruption. So I grumbled to myself and moved her things to her room, where she could be as messy as she wanted. Personal responsibility is a big deal to me, but life and God now teach her those lessons. I don't want to cut the number or length of her visits short because I make a big deal about her bad habit.

Katie's Thoughts

This may be the strong-willed child coming out in me, but I've noticed that usually when my mom stops nagging, I stop complaining. I remember when I noticed that she wouldn't complain about my stuff being everywhere, so I decided to pick it up. Once it wasn't an issue, I didn't need to make it one. Making issues out of things that don't matter can confuse both parties involved and lead to immaturity.

Keep Your Comments to Yourself

One of my mom's most needed and often used admonishments to my four sisters and me was, "Keep your comments to yourself." Nothing stirs up trouble faster than someone offering a comment that is not helpful. "Let no corrupt word proceed out of your mouth, but what is good for necessary edification, that it may impart grace to the hearers" (Ephesians 4:29). Think of the conflicts with your kids you would avoid if you kept your unedifying comments to yourself. The same is true when your child throws out something in conversation to bring about a certain response from you. If it's not on the list of nonnegotiables, don't respond. Katie does not share our political views, and we are not completely in step in our faith. If the conversation turns to these topics, I keep quiet or change the subject. She knows how I feel, and I know how she feels.

Donna learned this lesson quickly after Allison married Thomas. Donna advises parents, "No critical comments or questions that would lead to a critical comment." Donna knew Thomas's weak areas and steered clear of them in conversation. As a result, she said, her relationship with her daughter is sweet because Allison doesn't have to defend her husband.

Stay Involved

Ask about your child's friends while swerving around the immoral or illegal issues. Those kids are like your kids—they may be into messy stuff, but they're still kids needing love. Try to see them as people with their own hurts. Show genuine concern. How about inviting them over for a meal and sending them home with a loaf of homemade bread or cookies? Food speaks love and comfort. It's a little thing you can do to show the love of Christ.

Ask about anything positive in your child's life—school, work, interests, and so on. David said this was something his parents, Jan and George, did well: "They were pretty consistent about showing me that they cared about me personally. Not just by telling me, but by actively working towards it. Asking if I'd like to go places with them, trying to be involved in my life, conversing with me, asking about school and life."

Katie's Thoughts

I love getting mail from my family when I'm at college. I don't think a lot of parents still send their kids stuff, especially since most adults have Facebook. Parents think that a comment on their child's wall is the same as a care package. It's not.

I've really appreciated and taken for granted my parents always being available. My mom was always home after school or after I came home from a social event. I never had to wonder where my parents were or when they were getting home. They are supposed to do that with me! During high school, when I came home I usually spent the night in my room. But I always knew that if I wanted to talk, I would just have to walk down the hallway.

Never Say "I Told You So"

It's going to come. One day your child will walk in your door and say, "Mom, Dad, you were right. I shouldn't have (fill in blank)." Or they may say, "Mom, Dad, I did what you said not to and (fill in blank) happened." It may be a long time before you hear these words, but the temptation to say "I told you so" will be ever on your tongue. In fact, if you have the "I told you so" attitude, it oozes from your pores like the garlic from last night's Italian feast. Your child knows you're think-ing it. So don't. Quit thinking it. Instead, take on the role of cheerleader.

Be Your Child's Biggest Cheerleader

Gene and I are our girls' biggest cheerleaders. We encourage their good choices and successes—no matter what. We help them process the facts when they need to make a decision. We call it "keeping the wheels on the wagon." We help in a healthy fashion to keep them moving forward in a healthy fashion.

Katie hit an especially low point in her life after Mark broke off their engagement and placed the blame for the failed relationship on her. I'll let Katie share her story: "After the breakup I was pretty depressed, and that lead to a lack of interest in my future. The more I didn't think about what I was going to do, the less important it became. Eventually I was completely stuck."

One day we were hanging out at home and talking casually. I asked her, "Why don't you bite the bullet and take out the loans you need to finish college?"

She nodded and said, "Okay." This meant she would consider it, but she was not committing to anything.

I didn't think about it or mention it again. Then one day I had taken my mom out of town to visit her sister in a nursing home. My phone rang, and it was Katie. She excitedly explained to me that she had found a college that would be a great fit for her major, and she could transfer all her previous courses. I had no idea she was pursuing my idea of finishing college. With a little encouragement to boost her over a hard time, she was enrolled in a state university. Her little wagon was rolling down the road once again. She will graduate in one year at the age of twenty-six. She has persevered, and the end is in sight! A few months ago she said to me, "Mom, if you wouldn't have suggested for me to go back to school, I don't know what I would have done. I didn't have a plan."

Finishing her degree seemed like the next step. I didn't lay out a five-year plan for her. I offered her a suggestion and a way to make it happen. Then I stopped talking.

Katie's Thoughts

My mom's constant advice and encouragement helped me out of the hole I dug. Even such an obvious suggestion as college didn't occur to me. I had become blind to my options because of the focus on my problems.

Be the Real Deal

My efforts to show Katie (and all our girls) *I love you not matter what* has been more about me changing than her changing. This is the key to a meaningful relationship with our kids: we must let God help us be the parents they need. When we have a relationship with our kids, we have influence, a voice, an opportunity to help, and a way to show God to them. To be in a meaningful relationship, we must genuine. We must truly care about our kids, as opposed to trying to fix them or worrying about what others think.

Nathan says his parents did this well. "They were and are very concerned with who I am, and how I feel, and what I think," he says. Susan and George gave undivided time and attention to Nathan in order for him to know this about his parents.

Nathan goes on to say his parents led by example. He says, "They are the closest things to saints I know actually exist." Our lives must match or exceed our talk. Remember, our kids know us better than anyone. We can't fool them.

Also, be yourself with your kids. Let them see the real you. Are you funny? Then show them your humor. Even if they don't outwardly laugh at your jokes, they're laughing on the inside. When Katie was a freshman in high school, Gene started a joke with her that eventually became a family tradition. Gene picked Katie up from evening band practices every Thursday. My sister and her family (the Bells) live on a road that is on the way to the school. One night on the way home, just as they were approaching my sister's house, Gene said to Katie, "Katie . . ."

"What?"

"Looks like the Bells are getting ready for bed."

Not hilarious, I know, but the next week he did the same thing when they were close to her house.

"Katie . . ."

"What?"

"Looks like the Bells are getting ready for bed."

Only this time Katie responded with, "Oh, Dad!" He had her. She unsuspectingly fell for his silly joke. Gene continued this new tradition until Katie could drive herself. Then he started it with the other girls too. Most of the time the girls are not paying attention, Gene is able to sneak in the punch line, and they fall for the joke—for the umpteenth time.

Yep, it's silly, and you might be rolling your eyes. But that's okay because it's our family's joke. If you have a clever sense of humor, bless your kids with it. It will be one more sturdy block in the bridge to your child.

Are you artistic, creative, or musical? Invite your child to take a peek at your latest creation or listen to a piece you've been working on. I often send Katie blogs, cartoons, or books on the creative process, because it's an area where we connect—she with her art and me in my writing. What about sports? Or maybe you are an insightful, quiet listener. Ask a question that your child might like to answer— what are his thoughts about one of his interests? Then let him talk while he enjoys your *undivided attention*.

Nathan's parents did this well. Nathan shares, "My parents

paid attention to what I had to say and were genuinely interested and concerned. I want—and I think everybody wants—people to be around them that need them, and what they say is part of that. I believe it is actually a lot of that."

Involve Your Child in Family Life

As we discussed previously, Grace's college years were a difficult time for her and her parents. She lived in a constant state of making decisions her parents did not agree with, and these decisions were a wedge in their relationship. One thing her parents did that kept the door to relationship open was to treat her as a member of the family. "I felt like I was part of the family," she says. "I enjoyed my holidays at home. When it was time to celebrate, they didn't drag my baggage into it." By including our kids in normal family life, especially the fun parts, we create a safe zone for relationship to flourish. In this safe zone the seed of relationship grows. As the relationship grows, the parent gains more influence in the child's life—not to use in a manipulating way but in a healing way. Your child may come to you for advice. Offer biblical advice minus the sermon or scripture reference.

Look at the example of Jesus. He healed people physically—created a safe zone where their needs were met—and then they were ready to listen about how to be healed spiritually. This process may take months or years. God is working His plan, so we can relax and get into His stride. Take your time to build relationship with your child. You may not be the one to talk to your child about spiritual matters, but you may be preparing the ground for the person whom your child will listen to on these issues.

Speak Love to Your Child

Part of the change God worked in me was showing me how to speak love to Katie in a way that she could hear it and receive it. One time after I gave a presentation on this material, a mom asked, "I keep making lunch dates with my daughter, and she keeps standing me up. What do I do?" I responded, "Don't make any more lunch dates with her." Apparently eating lunch together was not a meaningful way to say *I love you no matter what* to this daughter. I challenged the mom to discover what actions spoke love to her daughter.

Katie's Thoughts

How Dad speaks love to me:

- Helps me with projects, engineering issues
- Lends/buys me tools and teaches me how to use them
- Talks to me about school and about his new jobs and hobbies

How Mom speaks love to me:

- Shows interest in my schoolwork and classes
- Talks to me on the phone while I'm at school
- Occasionally buys me a cute gift so I know she is thinking of me

Study your child. Think back to when he or she was young. What brought a smile to his face? What actions or words from you bring a positive response? Dr. Gary Chapman has written excellent books to help you learn to speak your child's love language. (See the list of resources at the end of this book.) Discover what speaks love to your child, and speak it fluently!

Maximize Technology

I'm definitely not proficient in technology, but I know enough to keep up. This is a simple idea, but so powerful. Use technology to build a relationship with your child. I text the girls with a thought or picture I think will make them smile. I send a quick question. Katie adores our cat, so I text her pictures of the cat doing something funny or cute. She loves it. How do I know? Recently she was looking through the pictures on her phone and made a humorous remark about all the cat pictures she had. That was her way of saying, *Thanks for including me, Mom.* Through the use of technology we build relationships with our kids without intruding into their lives. Essentially we are there for them when they have time for us. It works well for both parties.

A word of warning: remember your Facebook page is just that—*your* Facebook page. Use caution when posting anything about your children or their pictures. A misstep here has the potential to be more embarrassing than you chaperoning their prom, dancing while you're there, and wearing *your* senior prom clothes. I would hate for my Facebook faux pas to injure the relationship that I worked hard to build with my child. This goes for any form of social media.

To be effective, all our positive attempts at building a relationship must take place within the boundaries of emotional healthiness. Without healthy boundaries our efforts may further enable our kids' poor choices or our own issues we're working to overcome.

Love and Accept Your Child Where He Is

Jesus is the best role model of someone who loved and accepted people where they were. In fact, He still does. That's how you and I came into His family. He took us just as we are.

That's exactly what one of my pastors and his family did when they adopted their daughter at age fourteen. When Pastor Logan and his wife adopted Bethany, she had "virtually no spiritual life for the first ten years of life. She was a walking time bomb," said Pastor Logan. But they brought her into their home, where they already had three children, and loved on her. Gradually she is growing, maturing, and healing. Pastor Logan shares, "She is still very impulsive and gets angry easily, though she has come to appreciate the moral and spiritual framework that has spared her from many bad decisions that she could have made. The church has been a restrainer of negative behavior and has provided role models of exemplary behavior that keep Bethany from making poor choices."

Pastor Logan and his family showed Christ to Bethany by accepting her right where she was and loving her there. Their love earned a place in Bethany's heart, and she learned to be open to God and to change in her life. One last cool thing about Pastor Logan and his family—they recently adopted three siblings from Africa. They are growing the body of Christ by growing their family!

Our kids feel the same way as Bethany did. They give what they have for where they are in life, and that needs to be enough for us if we want to build relationships with them. If they show up for dinner but leave before dessert, let them know how glad you were to see them. Your genuine love and acceptance will work mightily to heal the relationship.

The Building Blocks for Healthy Boundaries

All healthy relationships have healthy boundaries. Just because our kids are our kids doesn't give us the right to overstep into their lives. Nor does it give our kids the right to take advantage of parents who love them and fear losing relationship with them.

Boundaries for the Parent

When our kids were babies and young children, everything about them was our business. Without us they could not have survived. But as they grew we released them in appropriate stages. They learned to work out friendships, communicate with teachers, manage their time, and so on. This development didn't happen without struggles and missteps. The wise parent knows mistakes are part of the growing process. Our toddlers learned to walk by falling before they found their stride, and our teens and young adult children will make many mistakes before they find their stride in making consistently good decisions. And as we let our toddlers fall and get back up, we must also let our grown kids fall and get back up in order to learn to do life and relationships well.

The following boundaries keep our relationships with our kids healthy and growing:

Don't push in where it's not your business. Many times Katie has asked my advice for a situation, but I don't hear how the situation turned out. It's okay. I did my part and offered the best advice I knew. It is up to her how or if she uses it. How she handles the situation is not my business. I resist the urge to ask follow-up questions that might cause friction. If she wants me to know, she'll tell me. In the areas of her life that affect our family life, we have firm, loving boundaries in place.

Don't let your curiosity or nosiness be a source of friction. If you truly need information about a sensitive subject, first try to get it from a confidential source. However, with adult kids, if you can't handle the truth, don't ask the question. Some things are better if we don't know. If you don't want to deal with what your child may say, don't go there.

Let their consequences be their consequences. Our youngest daughter, Kerry, received a speeding ticket. She deserved the ticket. We let her pay it from her savings account. This was her hard-earned babysitting money. I drove her to the courthouse to pay her fine. The boy ahead of us also had a fine to pay. He was about six feet two inches tall and had the build of a football player. He leaned over the counter like he owned the place while his dad counted out the money from his wallet. Then they left. Kerry was next. The clerk told her how much she owed. Her fair-skinned cheeks flushed as she sheepishly counted out the money from her wallet and humbly handed it to the clerk.

Who learned a lesson in the county clerk's office in those ten minutes? Both kids. The boy learned that his dad will clean up his messes. Kerry learned that her actions have consequences for which she is responsible.

Hold expectations loosely. Holding expectations loosely is a good rule for life in general, but especially with our kids. Katie has issues with being told what to do. Even asking if she will be home or will do something with the family can set her off. We've learned to hold our expectations loosely of her. If she comes, great. If she doesn't come, oh well. Make it easy on yourself and don't put yourself or anyone else in a position to depend on your child. Yes, I know, our children should be responsible and think of how their actions affect others, but they're not there yet. Accept it and move on.

Boundaries for the Child

The child also must honor healthy boundaries regarding the parents' lives, and parents must defend those boundaries. I recently spoke with a mom of a young adult son. He lived at home off and on. He was a source of irritation to everyone when he was there. I suggested they kick him out of the house. She said, "Well, his things are everywhere in the house. He won't take them with him."

I advised, "Gather up his things, put them in bags, and put them on the driveway or give them away."

She looked down and shook her head. She couldn't do it. Her fear kept her from being an effective parent in her son's life. She must enforce healthy boundaries that communicate, "Our home is our home, and if you want to be here you must follow house rules." If she refuses, then she inflicts unnecessary suffering on herself and her family. She also allows her son to stay a mess. Our healthy boundaries help our kids mature.

Money, money, money. Just like in marriage, the money issue in the parent-child relationship can be a deal breaker. Don't even start to add up how much your child owes you. Now is the time to come up with the money principles that will govern your future financial dealings with your child.

When Katie moved out, we told her we could not (and even if we could, would not) give her money for living expenses. If she was going to live on her own, she would be living on her own dollar. The only expense we have paid for Katie is her cell phone bill. She is on our family plan, and we want her to have the phone for safety. But we haven't turned our backs on her either. When Katie moved out of town to finish her degree, we have occasionally helped with the extras—gas money to come home, groceries, art supplies, and so on. These things kept her moving forward and were an encouragement to her. The few times we gave her money, we considered it to be a gift. It's the way we operate.

It's crucial for building a healthy relationship with your child that you come up with money principles that you will stick to. Ours is not the model for everyone; it's just what works for us. Devise a financial plan that will help your child and not enable him in any way. If it will be much different from the way you're handling money with him now, have a calm conversation about how money issues will work in the future. He may not like it. Katie used to think we gave her sisters more than we gave her, but Gene and I worked our plan for the best of each daughter.

Jan and George found themselves in a difficult situation and had to decide if they would stand by their words. One fall David disappeared. A few days later they received an e-mail from him saying his truck was at an airport two hundred miles from home. He was leaving, and they were not to try to find him. It was a tough time, and to add their worries, Jan and George were scheduled to leave on a mission trip halfway around the world. While they were away, David sent them a friendly e-mail, but he gave no clue where he was.

At Thanksgiving David contacted Jan and George. He was in Amsterdam. He ran out of money and did not have a work visa. He asked if they would send him money to fly home. With loving but firm resolve, Jan said, "This is a line in the sand—if you give in you lose the battle." They told their son no—they would not send him money.

David contacted a Christian school there and stayed with them through December. However, his visa expired on January 4. He contacted Jan and George again and said he must leave the country by January 4. Once again they said he would have to find another way home. Someone—they don't know who—bought him a ticket.

It was excruciating for Jan and George to let their son be destitute in a foreign country. But as Jan learned in Al-Anon, "You have to have strong boundaries. . . . You must define your boundaries, declare your boundaries to your child, and defend your boundaries." This is exactly what they did with David. When he called for money they had to decide if they would stand by their boundaries—and they did. After David came home, he continued to struggle, but he also started on a gradual progression toward finding and accepting help, healing, and healthy relationships. All because Jan and George defended their money boundaries.

Live your life well. As much as I believe we must be available for our kids, there are times when our presence will not help. In the above story, David would not have benefited if Jan and George had stayed home from their mission trip. The decision to go was right for everyone.

Lisa and James learned the same lesson throughout Greg's years of struggling. James encourages parents, "This is a marathon—not a sprint. You can't put all your emotional energy into this one child. You have to find your own life and life as a couple. Go to a movie and don't talk about the kid."

Sometimes our presence will help our kids, and sometimes they're going to do what they're going to do. Live your life. Don't let your life be defined by your child's decisions. If you have other children, it's not fair to them for your life to be defined by one child to the point that you can't enjoy life with the others.

Curfew. Curfew has been a major boundary issue at our house. Katie feels that because she has no one to report to at her apartment, she should have the same freedom when she is home. Because her mother physically cannot fall asleep if she doesn't know when one of her kids is coming home, and because the house belongs to Gene and me, we have the final say. We developed a compromise of requiring Katie to text us with her plans. She feels marginally intruded upon, and I have enough information to sleep. Bottom line here (and I don't use this often)—it is our house and our rules on this one.

The Cool You

Anytime my kids have thought me to be cool has been accidental on my part! Their evaluation of my coolness is as fickle as their teen hormones. Being the truly cool parent is being the parent who doesn't engage in the drama and traps set for him by his child. The child knows the cool parent loves him and where his parent's reasonable boundaries are. The child may not agree, but he has a measure of respect for the boundaries because he knows his parent is acting out of love and respect for him. The cool parent and his child have come to a place of agreeing to disagree. This provides the perfect venue for our next topic—giving your child room to grow.

8

The Learning Curve

Giving Your Child Room to Grow

Our house was unfinished for a few years when the girls were young. My dad and Gene built the house, and we finished it on the pay-as-you-go plan. While it was frustrating for me, it was perfect for raising arts-and-crafts girls. For most of Kelsey's preschool years, the living room and dining room floors were covered in paper—paper she played school with, made crafts with, and in general used for all kinds of fun. From the first day Kelsey talked, she played teacher. A few weeks ago she received her elementary education degree with academic honors. I like to think that by patiently allowing her paper mess, I contributed to that.

Kelsey isn't the only one who flourishes in a messy room. Last year Gene, Kelsey, Kerry, and I went to see Katie at college, where she lived in a studio apartment. She knew we were coming and was excited for our visit. She answered the door, and the four of us walked in and stood. And stood. Then we shuffled around a bit. There was no place to sit. Every piece of furniture, including the kitchen chairs, displayed Katie's artwork or art supplies. We made our way through as if touring the studio where a real-life artist lived and worked. And that's exactly what it was. Katie lived her artwork. She couldn't have been happier or prouder for us to make our way through the maze and comment on her accomplishments for the semester. That day I realized that all the neatness I tried to inflict on her (at least in her bedroom) was like a siphon stealing oxygen from her creative world. Her "messiness" was where she created and thrived as the person God made her.

Just as Kelsey and Katie needed space to flourish as the people God made them to be, our kids need space to grow, make mistakes, and (we hope) one day hear the voice of God calling their names. It would be nice if they stayed in the neat confines of a petri dish while growing, but that's not going to happen.

We think if only our children knew the truth, the big picture—the consequences, the positives *and* the negatives—they would make the right choice. But that is not reality. Nathan states this clearly to parents: "There is nothing my parents could have done to change my course/decisions. I was selfish and rebellious in the worst way. I could not have done it any other way."

David believes the same thing. "I would say, for the most part, that my parents did all they could to help me try and change my life course around," he reflects. "Sometimes, unfortunately, you just get stuck in a rut and have to see it out to fruition."

When Grace asked her parents to leave (in chapter 4), they were boarding a plane to return to the mission field in Europe. This began a period of silence between her and her parents. Her parents considered coming back, but their older, wiser mentors advised against it. Looking back, Grace agrees with their decision.

"It probably wouldn't have helped," she says. "It's God's timing. God kept doing His thing with me. It's a slow, gradual process."

As parents we want to fix our kids, but they are on their own coursse. God will use their paths for their good and His glory. During this time, we must hold our children loosely and give them room to work out their lives.

God's Plans Don't Always Look Like Our Plans

Keith, the youth leader with thirteen years' experience, often tells parents, "God is working His plan. What looks like a mistake is God's plan." In his experience, parents often try to control God instead of letting God work.

Keith started college with a major in history, even though his parents wanted him to pursue an education degree. His plan was to become a lawyer and then work for the FBI. His parents didn't agree with his decision, but they said, "Fine. It's your life— your decision." During his junior year he decided he wanted to change majors to education, which added two more years to his college career. However, the last three and a half years of his six-year college experience, he spent in campus ministry. If he had followed his parents' advice initially, he would have graduated in four years and totally missed his campus ministry experience. During his time in campus ministry he received his call for full-time ministry. Ministry took him to the mission field in Europe, where he met his wife. They have been in full-time ministry for nine years.

It's quite a story. Lots of zigs and zags. Through Keith's perspective it was an exciting journey with God. But put yourself in

Keith's parents' place. Lots of uncertainty. It must have been hard for them to resist the temptation to say "I told you so." But they were wise to give him room to grow.

Room for the Child to Grow

The parent who plays the part of the backstage director, correcting every little thing in the production of their child's journey, will remain in a state of disappointment and worry. His child will not grow into a confident, wise adult. Since he has not had the opportunity to learn from his mistakes, he stays dependent on the parent or latches onto someone else for security.

But the parent who takes a seat midway in the auditorium gives his child room to work things out. Yet he is still close enough to call up a direction when his child is about to step off the stage or when he asks for a prompt. This child learns to navigate the stage of his life, making mistakes and growing from them. He also learns there is no shame in doing so.

In this time of slow, gradual growth, there are many things we can do to help our kids and ourselves.

Back Off Without Cutting Off

James, as with many men he sees in his counseling practice, struggles in a different way than his wife, Lisa, does. "I see a lot of men more easily cut their losses. It hurts too much to have our son's poor decisions thrown in my face year after year," he says. "We need to back off without cutting off the relationship."

One way Gene and I have done that with Katie is not to blame her for the consequences of her poor decisions. Throughout our journey Katie trusted us more and more and, thus, called us for advice more often. By the tone of her voice and her opening statement—"Okay, I've decided . . ." or "Well, this happened . . ."—I could tell she was facing unpleasant circumstances from one of her poor decisions. Gene and I calmly listened to her share the details of the situation. As a journalist collects facts for a story, we asked questions for clarification. Then we subconsciously repeated the new mantra we adopted in the midst of the decisions we didn't agree with—*it is what it is*—to remind ourselves the issue at hand was what needed to be dealt with. It was not the time to place blame or rehash the if-onlys. The facts of her situation needed to be handled in a biblical way. We never tried to rescue her or help her find a loophole. We advised her how to proceed as if we would follow the advice ourselves. It was fact-based, unemotional, *this-is-the-next-thing-you-need-to-do* advice. We expressed to Katie how sorry we were that she was in the situation, but we didn't blame her or make her feel that she was the victim. We gave her solid advice in order to move her in a positive direction in her life.

We left it up to Katie whether she chose to follow our advice. We didn't offer a plan B just because she didn't like plan A. Rarely did we ask her how a situation turned out. It's part of backing off but not cutting off. We didn't take the burden of her consequences on ourselves; we didn't pressure her to respond in a certain way.

By keeping our critical comments to ourselves, we allow God and life to teach our children—often more clearly and quickly than we can. Katie's words from chapter 7 continue to echo through my brain: "I've noticed that usually when my mom stops nagging, I stop complaining. I remember when I noticed that she wouldn't complain about my stuff being everywhere, so I decided to pick it up myself. Once it wasn't an issue, I didn't need to make it one. Making issues out of things that don't matter can confuse both parties involved and lead to immaturity." Once we parents realize we are more effective in the middle section seats, our kids can hear the real director of their lives, God.

Tough Love

As our kids make decisions we don't agree with, one of the most beneficial things we can do for them and ourselves is to allow them to live out the consequences of their decisions. Here parents must proceed with a matter-of-a-fact attitude instead of a harsh one. This advice applies for any type of decision—preference, foolish, immoral, and illegal. As Keith's parents let him first choose a major they weren't crazy about, then switch to the one they recommended, they gave him room to figure out what was best for him. They kept building the relationship by not being naysayers.

When our kids' decisions veer into the foolish, immoral, and illegal, it is even more important to exhibit tough love, without forgetting the love part. The father of the prodigal son is an excellent example for us to follow (Luke 15:11–24). He let his son go to the distant country and live as he chose. The son spent his share of his father's estate and ended up destitute, wishing he could eat the pig's feed. (Take a minute and imagine this—your child spent his entire inheritance, so he is penniless. The last you heard from him, he was working for a farmer and eating the animals' feed because that's all he could manage.) The father didn't send a servant with a few dollars for fast food. The father stayed put on the homestead with a heart ready to receive his son when the son was ready. The father's arms were open wide so he could embrace his son when he returned. He could not have welcomed his son with arms crossed and a disapproving look on his face.

The tricky part for many of us is that our kids are living out their decisions in our homes or in our towns, so we are affected by the consequences of their actions.

After Deb's son, Brennan, spent a fair share of his inheritance on alcohol, drugs, legal fees, and counseling, she told him he couldn't live at home unless he went for help. As Deb explains, "We were living the same day over and over. We've got to do something differently." When Deb realized this, she was able to make the hard decision and give Brennan the ultimatum—get help or get out. It wasn't only for her, but for Brennan.

Brennan refused to get help, so he left home. Deb says, "He came to the end of himself—no work, no money, no friends." Finally he agreed to enroll in Teen Challenge[1]. Without that ultimatum, he would not have received the help he needed.

Cynthia and Frank also showed tough love to their daughter, Andrea. After the initial shock and hurt they felt when Andrea announced she was a lesbian, Cynthia and Frank worked to rebuild their relationship with Andrea and accepted their new normal. However, one condition was that Andrea could not bring girlfriends home with her to visit. They did not want to send the message to Andrea that they encouraged the homosexual lifestyle. Andrea was not happy about their stipulation, but she accepted it. They have been able to continue to show her love.

Jan and George came to the end of themselves with David. Like Brennan, he too had spent his portion of the estate on drugs, alcohol, counseling, and legal fees. The family felt they had nothing left to do, so they gathered family, friends, and the youth pastor for an intervention. Each person took turns reading their letters to David. Then George gave him the ultimatum—go to Teen Challenge or move out, with no cell phone or financial aid. David refused to go, so he moved out—on his own, with no help from George or Jan. After he moved they changed the locks on the house. The next day he came back to the house with his pillow but George and Jan would not let him stay. Instead, they called the youth pastor. He took David to lunch and back to his friend's apartment where he was staying.

Jan and George had done all they could for David. He refused to make positive changes in his life. Giving him the ultimatum was the best thing for him. After a few months, David decided to attend Teen Challenge. The tough love of his family brought him to a place where he could hear from God and decide to reach out for help.

The "Love" of Tough Love

In all of the toughness of tough love it's hard to find ways to still show love. Sometimes we must let the child stay in the distant country, but as I said, some kids just won't leave home.

Isaac was one of those kids. He tried his parents' patience over and over. He used and sold drugs. His parents finally kicked him out because they didn't want him to negatively influence their younger children. Isaac had no money and nowhere to go, so he lived in his car. You'll never guess where he parked his car at night—in a nearby church's parking lot, where his parents easily found him. Two or three evenings a week they brought him sacks of food so he wouldn't go hungry. His wise parents knew the importance of loving their boy, but they did not allow his sin back into their house. They were tough parents who showed love to their son—and to their other children by protecting them.

Another mom's tough love was exactly what her son needed to come to Christ. Andrew's mom asked her son to leave home because he was too much for her to deal with. I'll let Andrew's pastor tell the rest of their story.

> Andrew was a teenager when he became involved at our church. He was the product of a dysfunctional home. With no father figure in his life (he has never met his father), his mother threw him out of the house to live in a state-run facility for troubled youth. Andrew was alone and angry in a troubled world. God directed Andrew to our church, where immediately he began asking questions about God. We answered him in a loving and respectful way.
>
> He trusted Christ as a new believer within a year, and faced many temptations in his early Christian life. However, the body of Christ provided the structure of mentoring, guidance, job opportunities, Bible studies, and friendships that provided the right soil for the Word of God to thrive.

After five years of immersion in the life and relationships of the church, Andrew is a beautiful example of what it means when Christ makes all things new. Andrew's values, decisions, and affections are now firmly directly toward fulfilling his high calling in Christ. The church of Jesus Christ was the fertile field that allowed Andrew to have spiritual mothers, fathers, brothers, and sisters in Christ. Without the church, he was doomed to juvenile delinquency. But under the care of the church's teaching ministry, Andrew experienced the Word as a lamp to his feet and a light to his path.

Room for the Parent to Grow

It's easier to give our kids room to grow if we pursue the lives God has for us and take care of ourselves. Don't let your child's situation define you. The father of the prodigal son still ran his farm while his son was in the distant country. In fact, he may have worked harder to make up for the inheritance he gave to his son.

Give Yourself Room and Permission to Grow

James and Lisa, whose son Greg is still not to the end of himself, feed the homeless every Sunday morning with a group from their church. James advises other parents, "Find things in the present to invest yourself in. It contains the crisis."

I love this imagery. Immediately I picture an old-fashioned metal coffee can filled with dirt where a plant is growing. The plant and dirt represent your child and his life. The can sits in a hole in the yard, which represents your life. The plant's roots can spread only so far because they cannot poke through the metal can. The roots can't spread other plants like this one in the rest of your yard. Once we contain a difficult situation, we can live the life God has for us. As a result, we become better parents because we are not consumed by our children.

As our kids move into adulthood, they need to feel the responsibility of their own lives. When they see they are no longer consuming our lives and the safety net of Mom and Dad is now gone, they must decide to make better choices or endure the consequences.

In both his ministry and in his own family, Keith has seen the benefits of parents who refused to be their children's safety net. In regard to substance abuse, when the parent has tried to help and intervene in every way possible he advises, "Don't do any-thing. Let them crash and burn. Being a safety net is not helpful."

Seek Your Own Help

Jan and George went to Al-Anon early in David's struggle with drugs and alcohol because they had no idea how to handle the situation. At the time they didn't know anyone going through a similar experience. At first Jan didn't want to go because of her pride, but there she learned truths about her situation and her son. This information helped her deal with everyday reality. God used Al-Anon to help her move forward. She learned to trust God with her son, and be the mom her son needed. She encour-ages parents to educate themselves on whatever issues overtake their children's lives. It's part of our growth process as parents and keeps us from a downward spiral of hopelessness.

Cooperate with God's Work in You

God allows the painful circumstances in our lives to change us into the image of His Son. Your situation with your child is no different. While you give your child room to grow, give yourself the same gift. Seek God and ask Him what He wants to teach you in this situation and how He wants you to change. Jan is eager to share how she has changed for the better. "I have received so many gifts—compassion, self-esteem," she says. "I like myself . . . I have relaxed from being rigid—having to have things go my way. I now have deep friendships."

As I try to decide on a tidy sentence about God's work in me with which to end this section, I cannot come up with one. God is forever working on me—plowing up what I once thought was the only way and showing me it wasn't sacred at all. He continually helps me to embrace my kids' preferences even though they're not the same as mine. He helps me keep perspective on lesser issues so when I need to give a parental word on an important issue the girls are ready to listen. And you know what? My kids do the same with me. They embrace my preferences and celebrate my victories. They don't cringe when I talk about healthy eating and fitness with their friends. They aren't embarrassed if I serve a heart-healthy meal to their friends for supper. I do my best to cooperate with God as He makes me into the mom they need. He is blessing me with kids who enjoy being in relationship with me (some days more than others!).

A Word About Your Marriage

As I talk with parents about their kids' decisions they don't agree with, I am surprised at how often the subject of how this problem affects their marriages comes up. I don't know why I am surprised. Of course, any issue that brings deep emotion and sometimes life-changing consequences will have the propensity for disagreements. Each parent brings his or her own history to parenting. Each parent has a different personality and, mixed with the child's personality, will produce different chemistry with the other parent. If anything can try to "put asunder" the "one flesh" God "joined together" (Matthew 19:6 KJV), it's disagreements on how to parent, especially when the child veers from the norm in his decisions.

Jan and George were drawn closer as a couple through the difficult times of parenting David. She remembers, "George and I leaned on each other. Our marriage made it through everything by God's grace and strength." Jan shares a list of things that helped their marriage:

- Affirm one another—build each other up. This helps when you feel discouraged by your child's behavior. Try to tell each other things you are thankful for in each other and in other parts of your life.
- Talk about something other than your problems—how your day was, how you have grown spiritually, how exercise is going, and so on.
- Laugh. Spend time with friends who help you laugh. Just act silly. You both may need breathing time—doing nothing about situation—for answers to come. As parents, doing nothing can sometimes work magic with your child's learning.
- Talk about situations, boundaries, feelings, and so on.
- Have someone else beside you who listens and is wise. This helps to not put the whole burden on each other.
- Go to church together and serve others. We serve at a homeless breakfast together.
- Get professional help. We have an excellent counselor who understands our child's issues.

Oh, if only all couples made an effort to draw closer in this situation. As Cynthia shared, her marriage was a struggle from the beginning. When Andrea told her parents of her decision to live the lesbian lifestyle, Frank was just as hurt and saddened as Cynthia was, but his reaction was very different. He told Andrea that unless she changed she couldn't come home. Cynthia says, "I could not be absent from one of my children's lives. I still love her. She's still my child." This conflict became another struggle in Cynthia's marriage. "For years Andrea was our only topic of conversation. Her situation always came up."

The kids' decisions were also a source of friction in Deb and her husband's marriage. Deb's first marriage to Brennan's dad ended because of her ex-husband's alcohol and drug abuse. Brennan followed in his dad's footsteps, so by the time Deb and her second husband, Allen, were married she knew the signs. Allen's son, Rory, started drinking in high school. Deb immediately saw the changes in Rory that she had seen in Brennan. She spoke to Allen, but he refused to accept her warning as truth. "He wanted to think he had a close relationship with him," Deb says. When Rory was a senior he received a DUI. She continues, "He latched on and drinking and drugs became a way of life." Her husband thought Rory was going through a phase. This disagreement caused further stress in their marriage.

Donna and Bob have different personalities, which caused friction in their marriage when Allison pushed her limits. Donna says, "If you don't have the same parenting style, it's easy to blame the spouse because you would have done it differently. Satan uses blame and guilt—such as, 'If only my husband would have done this . . .'"

It may seem like this issue is different from the other issues in your marriage because your child's well-being is at stake. But if you can deal with this problem as you do with the others in your marriage, you will come to a better plan for your child more quickly than if you fight it out.

Julie and Marty did not agree at all on how to deal with Aaron's dishonesty. Julie explains, "Marty and Aaron are so much alike, so Marty was hard on Aaron. Marty and I were on totally different wavelengths. When he wanted to discipline Aaron, I got in between them. I was more worried about protecting their relationship than [about] what God was doing." How insightful of Julie to understand that it's not her job to protect Marty and Aaron's relationship. Their relationship is not her (or any mother's) responsibility. The responsibility for the relationship lies with the two people in it—in this case, father and son. She also realized that God was working on something bigger than a disagreement between father and son. By butting heads with Marty, Aaron would learn how to communicate with a man as a man—no more hiding behind his mama's skirt.

Give Your Spouse Space to Grow

Your spouse is on his or her own journey as well. He or she needs whatever time it will take to come to terms with the situation and consider how to best proceed. It took a little while longer, but Allen finally accepted the reality that his son had a drug and alcohol problem. Then as a unified couple, Allen and Deb tried everything—counseling, boundaries, consequences. Nothing affected Rory. Finally the turmoil in their home was so intense, Allen asked Rory to leave.

God was at work in Allen. Deb had to be patient as God worked on Allen while she continued in her own growth.

Seek Information as a Couple

Jan shared how helpful it was to become educated about her son's addiction. Cynthia also found education helpful in her marriage. "We handle it differently now," she says. "We have a lot more info. I connected with Focus on the Family. Through the years Frank and I have tried to love Andrea as best we can."

Part of our growth is processing as a couple what we learn about our children's problems. We hear or read the same material and then discuss it and decide how we will live it. This helps us grow as parents and also deepens our marriage. The most important thing in our marriages and in our parenting is for us to do the best we can—not demanding perfection but moving forward in relationship and with the Lord.

Be Open to a New Perspective

While you are learning and processing, you might see that your spouse has a different perspective than you do. Because of our life experiences and personalities, Gene and I had different perspectives on how to approach Katie's decisions. Over the years we have both learned the value in listening to each other and considering our children's points of view. We discuss the situation and do what we think is best. Just in case you're about to write us off as Mr. and Mrs. Perfect Communicators, don't. Communication has been one of our major areas to grow in during our marriage. I communicate too much, and Gene not as much as I do. After twenty-seven years we've learned a little but are still very much in process.

God has given your child the two of you for her parents. That means you both are needed in her life. Your insights are valuable and so are your spouse's. Lay aside any marital issues and honestly hear your spouse, evaluate the conversation, and then do what is best for your child.

Find Good, Professional Help

As in other areas of life, when the problem is bigger than the resources you have, find good, professional help. We hire professionals for every other area of life (medical, financial, mechanical—and where would I be without my dry cleaners?). Can we admit we need help and guidance with the most important personal relationships in our lives? Ask someone you trust for a recommendation. If the first counselor or pastor doesn't seem like a good fit, keep looking. Just because a counselor is a Christian doesn't mean he will give good guidance. Be savvy, trust your gut, and seek until you find the right one.

The stories shared are for your encouragement and consideration. As Deb wisely states, "There is no formula. We must be willing to try different things." And so it will be with each family. Seek God's direction on what He has for you and your child. We'll give each other the gift of grace as we do so.

9

Everybody Is Talking

Knowing with Whom to Share What

High school Sunday school class was tough for Katie. She asked Gene and me if she could come to Sunday school with us. Of course we said yes. Why wouldn't we? Every week she heard sound biblical teaching and had the opportunity to interact with and observe mature believers—for the most part.

However, I was not prepared for the inquiries from some people in our Sunday school class. They wondered why Katie was in class with us and not in the high school class. I wanted to let them know how I was thankful she was in *any* Sunday school class, hearing the Word taught. I wanted them to understand that at this particular time, the high school Sunday school was not a safe place for Katie because of the cliquey attitude of some of the girls. I wanted to explain many things, but I didn't. This situation quickly showed me that unless other parents have experienced their children making decisions they don't agree with, they might have a hard time understanding our situation. As a result their comments might not be helpful. I decided then that I needed to wisely choose those with whom I shared our journey. In fact, I decided from that point forward I would not share with anyone until I had proof he or she cared for my daughter and would not judge her.

When Jan talks about her experiences with other people, she laughs and says, "My church was the worst place to go. I tried to avoid the bathroom because that is where I got cornered." How sad! What are we doing to each other? This is not the way the body of Christ cares for its members. Church should be a safe place to receive love, acceptance, and encouragement for the difficulties of life. Jesus teaches us the importance of showing love to each other: "By this all will know that you are My disciples, if you have love for one another" (John 13:35). Not only do we bless each other when we show love, but it is a major way we show Christ to the world. Why would anyone want to be part of something that chews up and spits out those who are hurting or struggling? The way we love each other in difficult times is by being "Christ with skin on" to other believers and the world.

Unfortunately, many times, we receive the opposite—judgment. Jesus speaks of this attitude in Matthew 7:1–2: "Judge not, that you be not judged. For with what judgment you judge, you will be judged; and with the measure you use, it will be measured back to you." Here *judge* is defined as "to try, condemn, or punish."[1] Yet in 1 Corinthians 2:15 we are told, "But he who is spiritual judges all things, yet he himself is *rightly* judged by no one." In this context judged is defined as "to investigate, determine, ask, question."[2] What's different is the attitude. We do not sit as judge and jury, ready to condemn and punish. That is not our job. No one wants to be analyzed and condemned, so why do we do this to others? Don't we all have enough garbage for others to pick through, and wouldn't we appreciate it if they didn't?

Jesus commands us in John 15:12, "This is My commandment, that you love one another as I have loved you." Our God, the one and only true God, is love and loves us so much—"And so we know and rely on the love God has for us. God is love" (1 John 4:16 NIV). The apostle John wrote these words in a letter to Christians all over Asia Minor. He tells his readers that they should rely on God's love every day in their Christian life.

When John wrote this letter, Christianity was still a young religion. The world at that time was not heavily populated with other believers or Bible-preaching churches. The early Christians needed to know that God loved them and that, because of His faithful love for them, He could be trusted to care for them daily. Notice what helping verb is not used by John in this verse—*can*. John (under the inspiration of the Holy Spirit) does not say, "And so we know and *can* rely on the love God has for us." He doesn't make it optional for the believer to rely on God's love. The early believer *needed* God's love to live each day.

Believers today (especially those in developed Western countries) put God's love on the top shelf as an optional ingredient in their day. We don't understand and live by the truth that God's love for us is our lifeblood, not just for eternity but for today. Because we've forgotten this fact, we don't live in God's joy, nor do we let "the love of God [that] has been poured out in our hearts by the Holy Spirit who was given to us" (Romans 5:5) flow through us to others.

In this love-starved state we focus more enforcing God's rules. We don't rely on God's love for ourselves, and we certainly don't pass it on to others we feel are less worthy—our kids or other parents' kids who are making poor decisions. We waste our most precious resource for this life—God's love! In the center of God's love we are accepted and cherished; we have peace; we are free from our past.

Why, then, don't we as followers of Jesus Christ live in a way that exhibits God's love to the world, like

- a spectacular fireworks show?
- a warm quilt on a frigid night?
- the aroma of fresh-from-the-oven cinnamon rolls and coffee?
- a bear hug that says *I'm here for you*?
- an ear-to-ear smile from a loved one just because you walked into the room?

Why? Because we don't rely on God's love for ourselves. We forget that Jesus said, "This is My commandment, that you love one another as I have loved you" (John 15:12). It's His plan for how His body is to operate. There is no plan B for the body of Christ. If we want to show the world our Lord and fulfill His plan for us, we must love others as He loved us.

Living in the center of God's love equips us to deal graciously and wisely with people's comments. We learn to seek out the people we need to journey with and continue to build relationship with our kids.

Dealing with Other People's Comments, Disapproval, and Opinions

The father of the prodigal son didn't have to go far to hear negative comments. When the son came home, the father threw a huge party for him. The father's older son returned from working in the field and asked about the party in progress at his house. The servant explained the good news.

> "But he was angry and would not go in. Therefore his father came out and pleaded with him. So he answered and said to his father, 'Lo, these many years I have been serving you; I never transgressed your commandment at any time; and yet you never gave me a young goat, that I might make merry with my friends. But as soon as this son of yours came, who has devoured your livelihood with harlots, you killed the fatted calf for him'" (Luke 15:28–30).

Wow! Don't hold back. Tell your dad how you really feel.

The Bible doesn't specifically describe the older brother's attitude toward his brother when he was gone, so let's play out this family dynamic by imagining they are a "normal" family with "normal" sibling rivalry and "normal" issues. I can't imagine the older son holding in this bitterness for the extended time his brother was in the distant country. No, I imagine the older son started keeping score before the younger son left. When the younger son started doing life his own way, the older son pulled out his scorecard. Perhaps he muttered negative comments about his brother within earshot of his father. Did he give his father a verbal jab every time the younger son messed up? The younger son's poor decisions fueled the sibling rivalry that existed naturally. And this doesn't take into account the comments the neighbors and fellow churchgoers may have offered.

The father responded to his older son by reminding him of how much he loved him and explaining the reality that his brother was once dead, but now was "alive again." That's all the Bible tells us. No cajoling or trying to convince the older brother to forgive.

However, most people who offer unsolicited comments are not in your inner circle and do not need (or deserve) an explanation from you regarding your child's decisions. They are on a need-to-know basis—and most of them don't need to know.

Dealing with Comments from Parents of Your Child's Partners in "Crime"

Some of the most shocking comments may come from *other* parents of kids making decisions they don't agree with. When David crashed the family van after drinking and smoking marijuana with friends, Jan and George called the parents of the other kids in the van to let them know what happened. Many of the parents were in denial that their children could be involved in alcohol and drugs—they said that maybe Jan's son was drinking and doing drugs, but their children never would. What a dangerous posture—to not believe (or to be unwilling to consider) that your child could ever do something foolish, immoral, or illegal. We all struggle with our sinful human nature and are capable of any sin.

Julie, Aaron's mom, warns parents about thinking their children would never disappoint them: "[I was] assuming I knew my child well enough to recognize if he was lying, but I didn't. There were warning signs. It should have clicked, but it didn't. He got really good at lying through all this." Aaron waited until two days before his supposed graduation to tell his parents the truth—that he had not been in classes for two years. Julie recalls, "He waited until his back was to the wall! But he did confess and was very remorseful and humiliated. There were a lot of tears."

To deny that our children are incapable of deceiving us or turning from the way we raised them is more than naive; it's irresponsible. I know we want to give our kids the benefit of the doubt, but as a Christian counselor shared with me, "I always ask the question, 'Is it possible?'" Is it possible your child has been hiding something from you?

Even after you accept the truth about your child, remember that others may not be ready to do the same about their children. Jan and George did the right thing, the responsible thing. If you are in the position to do the same, be ready for the parent who refuses to hear and then places the blame on you and your child. Be gracious, but do not assume responsibility for something that is not your or your child's problem.

Dealing with Comments from Those Not on the Need-to-Know List

Jan and George and their family live in a small town. News of David's wreck and its cause raced through town almost faster than the police report was filed. Their phone began ringing. People called to give unsolicited advice or just to say "shame on you."

Parents, you do not owe these people an explanation or discussion regarding your family. Jesus never took the bait of the self-righteous religious community. One excellent example is in John 8:3–11: "The scribes and Pharisees brought to Him a woman caught in adultery" (v. 3). Allow me a sidebar here to suggest the intent of the woman's accusers. It takes two to commit adultery. What was the man's part in this behavior? How did these religious creepers know the woman would be with the man? It appears this woman was set up. She was definitely used to set a trap for Jesus (v. 6). Your accusers may try to set you up as well.

This religious bunch laid the snare: "Teacher, this woman was caught in adultery, in the very act. Now Moses, in the law, commanded us that such should be stoned. But what do You say?" (vv. 4-5) Jesus responded masterfully: he "stooped down and wrote on the ground with His finger, as though He did not hear" (v. 6). He not only refused to take the bait—he didn't even appear to hear them! Oh, they must have burned at His dismissal of their perfectly presented case against this woman. Verse 7 says they kept after Him to answer them. Unfortunately, your accusers will also persist in their self-righteousness and their need to help you and your "poor" child.

Finally Jesus stood up and turned the focus back on them. "He who is without sin among you, let him throw a stone at her first," he said (v. 7). He did not defend her. He did not discuss the Law and its application (which He could have done with full authority). He calmly showed grace to the woman and gave the self-righteous religious community an opportunity to do the same. Then He did something most of us, especially us parents who don't want our kids to be misunderstood, find almost impossible. He stopped talking: "And again He stooped down and wrote on the ground" (v. 8). That ended the discussion of the woman's sin. No explanation. He stopped talking and, in effect, changed the subject. He went back to writing on the ground. I've heard clever suppositions regarding what He wrote, but no one truly knows. We only know that He did not engage the critics.

Thus He closed the curtain on the scene the religious righteous tried to create. "Then those who heard it, being convicted by their conscience, went out one by one, beginning with the oldest even to the last" (v. 9).

Jan followed Christ's example. She advises, "Have a response ahead of time . . . something like, 'I'm so thankful God's at work in his life.' Then walk away." She learned that we "can't tell everyone everything. They don't deserve to know." Your child is still your child, and part of your job is to protect him—not from his consequences but from those who would feed on his situation to satisfy their own immoral appetite for a "choice morsel" of gossip (Proverbs 18:8, 26:22 NIV). You do not owe anyone an explanation. As Jan advised, prepare your response and stick with it. You can do this. Preserve your emotional energy for your child and the other parts of your life. Don't let it be siphoned by those who are not on your need-to-know list.

Your Need-to-Know List

One of the blessings of walking with our children on his journey is meeting amazing people who love and accept us and our children. These people show Christ to us. They are the "aroma of Christ" (2 Corinthians 2:15 NIV) to us and to the watching world. They give us the support, encouragement, advice, and love we need to continue in our journey.

Put Other Parents on that List

Gene and I were invited to a friend's home for an evening with the "old people" of our church. The church was so young that Gene and I (ages sixty and fifty, respectively) were considered some of the oldest people in the church. After dinner we shared a little about our journeys with God. The common thread that ran through almost everyone's story was a child who was making decisions they didn't agree with. As each parent shared, the night air on my friend's deck grew sweet with the aroma of love and acceptance that poured from the rest of the group. Most of us knew the heartache of a child not walking with the Lord, and that comes from the hurtful responses of others. But this group was different. In this group we felt love and acceptance, not only for ourselves but for our kids.

Deb, who walked this journey with her son Brennan and her stepson Rory, encourages parents to find other parents who are kindred spirits and will be there for you. She adds, "Judge wisely." Be careful about how much you share and how quickly you share it. Often you can tell if a parent is safe by how she talks about her own child. Degrading remarks about her child aren't a good indicator she will be gracious with you and your child.

Deb also challenges parents to know when to speak up and share their experiences with other parents in order to help them. She said, "Encouragement is so important." There is no sure way to know who is safe to share with and who will turn on you after you offer encouragement. Pray for the Lord's leading, and if the other parent doesn't receive your advice well, show grace and back off.

Put Professionals on that List

Nathan's poor decisions led to legal consequences. One of Gary's friends was a lawyer and was always available to advise and help Nathan. Nathan valued his help and friendship. Trusted professionals are a valuable resource for you and your child. Parents, pray for God's leading here and don't be too proud or hesitant to ask someone to pour into your child. The list of possible helpers is extensive: lawyer, doctor, counselor, police officer, clergy, rescue mission staff, teacher, coach, and so on.

The point is not for these professionals to get your child out of his consequences but to give him the real help he needs. Keith shared an experience of a young woman who bought "a pit of a house." Her parents did not want her to buy any house and certainly not that one. Maybe had they not been so against the purchase of a house they might have had a voice in which house their daughter bought. (Remember, without relationship we have nothing.) With the "pit of a house" now hers, she could not live in it until major renovations were finished. The men of her church came to her rescue and made her house livable on her budget.

Has your child proven herself ready for a real job? Who do you know would give her an opportunity to move forward and would still be gracious to her and you if she fails?

Put Church on that List

The church in which Gene and I were considered some of the oldest people is also the church many of the kids of those same parents tried after making decisions their parents didn't agree with. This church probably doesn't look like the church you grew up in. Everyone comes in jeans, even the pastor. The music is loud—rock concert loud. Coffee is served and welcomed in the sanctuary. Many of these churchgoers (also including the pastor) have tattoos. The Word of God is preached. The pastor gives voice to the kids' hurting hearts. The kids come even though they're teetering between the church world and their world of poor choices. And they bring their friends. They sing to the Lord loudly and with arms in the air (really in the air, none of that half-elbow bend stuff). They marry. They have babies. Lots of babies. Strollers line the back of the sanctuary. And the Word of God is preached.

Jan and George left the church where they raised their family to come to this church. They switched churches so they could bring other hurting parents and their kids, and their own son, to a church where they might feel more comfortable.

Remember Connie and Robert's son, Jeremy, who did drugs with his friends at their house? Jeremy still smokes marijuana with his friends when he can sneak it. Guess where he wants to go to church. That's right—this church. Before you pull out your Pharisaical soapbox and say something like, "Hey, we can't let those kids keep making poor choices and come to church like nothing's going on," think. Why not? Back to our self-examination. Do we go to church all cleaned up on the inside? And didn't Jesus have a word about this for the Pharisees? "And when the Pharisees saw it, they said to His disciples, 'Why does your Teacher eat with tax collectors and sinners?' When Jesus heard that, He said to them, 'Those who are well have no need of a physician, but those who are sick'" (Matthew 9:11–12). These kids don't bring their drugs to church. They don't come drunk. They come with hearts to hear and worship, and that's what they do.

Would a change in church interest your child? Are you hanging on to a church that barely works for you and hasn't worked for your child in years?

Put Friends Who Have Been There on that List

I was surprised when I discovered which of my friends had rough times in their relationships with their parents because of their decisions. I remember one day a few years ago sharing with one of my closest friends about a rough spot in my relationship with Katie. She compassionately listened and then said something I did not expect. With the same compassion she gave me, she explained how she identified with Katie and all she was going through. She shared some of her past with me—including living with her boyfriend and the emotional consequences of that decision—things I previously had no idea about. She challenged me to understand where Katie was in life. I felt more endeared to her as a friend because she shared so intimately with me—but even more so because she unveiled a tender spot in her heart for my daughter. She didn't give a hint of criticism or a judgmental attitude.

My friend from chapter 1 (whose comment "I just knew" became my parenting mantra) has calmly and graciously throughout the years reassured me in my parenting and in Katie's progress in her journey. This can be a lonely journey, and after a while it's easy to let other people's preaching (not God's Word, but theirs) pick away at what you know to be truth. Every so often I have shared with my friend how Gene and I are doing in our relationship with Katie. I lay out my doubts and insecurities. She reassures me we're on the right path. Sometimes we need someone who's been there and back to reassure us we're still going the right way.

Katie's Thoughts

My aunt Lisa was really supportive when I was jobless and going through hard times, especially during the breakup of my engagement with Mark. Not only did she hire me to help her around the house and with her kids, but she listened to me, even when I was making immature decisions. She didn't judge me. Even now, she always speaks to me like an adult, offers suggestions, and shares her personal experiences.

I am so careful about sharing my kids' decisions with others that when I answer the question, "What are you currently writing?" many people are surprised. Then they ask, "Have you had experience with this?" Rely on God's love for you, and He will give you graciousness for those who need it and guide you to those who will walk with you and your child on this journey.

10

Happy Ending

Writing the Rest of the Story and Liking It

By now you've figured out that your life and your child's life will not be as you imagined—even if the issue is only that your child's preferences are not your preferences. You've learned that the equation A + B = C is not always true. There is much hope for parents and their kids as both continue on this lifetime journey. Once again, I want to remind you our goal is not to bring our kids to the Lord. That's not our job. We want to build relationship with them for this life. By doing so we clear the way for them to return to the Lord when He works in them and brings them back.

Will you make the decision to be a part of your child's life even if it's not what you planned or hoped for? We are having a ball being part of Katie's life. She spent last weekend with us. Gene helped her with concrete and metal work for a sculpture assignment. Katie and I discussed a book on artistic inspiration that I sent her. We ate out as a family to celebrate Kerry's college scholarship. It was a nice weekend—one that would not have happened had I remained the My-Way-or-the-Highway Mom I once was. Not every part of our weekend was perfect, but that's life. So will you be in your child's life, celebrating the good and hanging in there through the difficult?

Bank on Your Earlier Deposits

When our kids are making poor choices, it's easy to believe that everything we did for them has been forgotten. But this is not so.

A couple of years ago the art program at Katie's college sponsored a trip to the Art Institute of Chicago. Touring this amazing art museum was like drinking from a fire hose for Katie. She loved every minute but was overwhelmed by the inspiration, talent, and excellence of the collections. After the tour Katie and her friends ate at a nearby restaurant. Katie excitedly started a discussion about what pieces inspired her. Her friends, however, were distracted. Seated next to them was a family celebrating their small child's birthday. Katie noticed they were having a typical birthday celebration—pictures, cake, gifts, and lots of love and attention on the birthday child. Katie thought, *Cute, but no big deal.* Her friends also noticed the family's party and couldn't take their eyes off them. Seeing her friends were no longer listening to her, Katie tried to get their attention. Both had tears in their eyes.

"I never had a birthday party," said one of the friends.

"Me either," agreed the second friend.

Katie expounds on the story: "About then the waitress took pictures for the family. This brought on even more moaning."

"Oh, I never had pictures taken," cried the first friend.

By then the excitement of the Art Institute had been replaced by the emptiness and ache in Katie's friends' hearts. However, Katie glanced at the party and thought, *Been there. Done that. I'm ready for what's next.* Throughout her life we filled her heart with love and memories. One way was by celebrating her birthdays with friends, family, food, and pictures. The little love bank in her heart was full of our deposits of love. She relied on these, even took them for granted, as she lived her decisions—the good ones and the not-so-good ones. She knew we loved her no matter what. Her friends' hearts had not been filled up. They did not have a large balance to rely on.

Most of us wish we had loved on our kids more. But know that the love you deposited into your child's heart is still there, and she knows it. Let's build on that.

It's Not All About You

Remember, when it comes to parenting an older child, it's not all about you. Your child's life is his life—his choices, his consequences. Roll the burden of that realization where it belongs—on the Lord and your child. Several of the moms I interviewed talked about this.

- Donna—"We're fooling ourselves to think it's all up to us. We're responsible [for doing] what we can."
- Deb—"I can't blame anyone. My son made those choices. I love my son, but I was able to separate myself from him. He's God's son, too."

- Jan—"I had to learn that the outcome is not in my hands."
- Cynthia—"You're trying to resolve [the problem] and you realize you can't. It's not in your hands. It's in God's hands."
- James—"I can't fix [the situation]. I will not enable it. I will love my child."

James's words perfectly state what we're doing in this book. We cannot fix our children or their lives. We are to love them but not help them continue in their poor choices. It is our privilege to encourage them in good decisions.

Be on Your Child's Team

It means so much to our kids that we are for them continually. David shared that about his parents, Jan and George: "The most helpful thing my parents did was to come alongside and [work] with me as a team rather than stand out front and try to lead me." It's one way we show them we love them no matter what.

James finds maintaining this attitude challenging too: "We lose sight of the good and start looking for the bad. 'Well, he's late.' But we miss that he did come. Keep comments positive." Lisa adds, "Let him see my heart is toward him."

I've said this throughout the book because it is vital to building a relationship with your child and because it is difficult, especially at the beginning. Look for little ways to encourage and show love. Then continue to take cues from your child and encourage him. Katie called last weekend and shared about her hard week. After I got off the phone, I told Gene about our conversation. He said, "Let's go see her tomorrow afternoon." He immediately called her. She was thrilled. We took her out for lunch and a little shopping. By 4:00 p.m. she was refreshed and ready for another week of school! It was a little thing that made a big impact on her.

Live in the Moment

Any parent who thinks she has her kids' lives under control is delusional. For those of us who are daily reminded by our kids that we don't have, nor ever have had, their lives under control, living in the moment is our oxygen. Allowing the past to take up residence in our guest room is torture. Looking ahead to the future brings unnecessary worry. Living in the moment is where God wants us.

Jesus teaches us this clearly in Mathew 6:25–34. He challenges us worrisome parents, "Who of you by worrying can add a single hour to his life?" (v. 27 NIV). The same goes for our kids' lives as well. All of our worry will not change a thing in our lives or our kids' lives.

Jesus ends this section of teaching with, "Therefore do not worry about tomorrow, for tomorrow will worry about itself. Each day has enough trouble of its own" (v. 34 NIV). We sure have learned that, haven't we? Living in the present that God has given us is the safest place to be.

Deb shares a powerful truth that the enemy doesn't want us to believe: "Most of the 'should've' wouldn't change anything." Beating ourselves up over what we should have done differently keeps us stuck. She ends her interview with, "All we can do is live this day forward." That is what Jesus teaches too.

Jan encourages families to have fun. "We recently took a vacation for a change of scenery and refreshment. It helped gain perspective and strength. Even though we are not on the same page with our son's choices right now, we are family and had a great time eating out, playing games, and enjoying the ocean." She challenges parents to enjoy what today brings: "Live one day at a time. Live in the moment. Your kids can go back." As with all life, nothing is guaranteed and God gives us only the present to enjoy, but Jan doesn't want parents to live in fear. For the times our kids are not making good choices, Jan shares, "Whether or not our kids change, we have to enjoy the good things in life."

Keep Praying

I know we've talked about prayer, but we must not ever forget this is where we are most powerful—laying our kids in the hands of their loving Father.

Look back at our friend the father of the prodigal son (Luke 15:11–31). Notice why the son repented and returned home: "When he came to his senses, he said, 'How many of my father's hired men have food to spare, and here I am starving to death?'" (v. 17 NIV). "When he came to his senses"—the son repented when he finally figured out it was the best choice. The most influential thing we can do is pray to God for our kids to come to their senses. In God's time, in the quiet of their hearts while they're sitting in their pigsties, He will talk to them and give them the opportunity to come to their senses. This is how we best pray for our kids: "Please, God, bring them to their senses!" That's what they need most, isn't it? Then all the truth they've heard and learned from experience will make sense, and they'll make better choices (some of which you might still not agree with, but you're the cool parent now).

Donna came to this realization. "We think we can inspire our kids to fear the Lord," she says. "It's only the Lord who can inspire them to fear Him. Praying diligently for adult children has been a blessing. Keep diligently praying for the most important thing in life. Recognizing that I can't move my kids to follow God keeps us on our knees."

Cynthia talks about how her prayers for Andrea have changed: "In the beginning, I prayed for some man to come and sweep her off her feet. Then I prayed for protection and guidance. Now I just want her to have the love of Jesus—to have her eyes and heart open."

I, too, pray for protection and guidance while my child is in the distant land—whether it is for an extended stay or a short visit caused by a lapse in good judgment. I want her to learn what she needs to learn but not experience unnecessary evils while she's there.

Reach Out to Others

As we discussed in chapter 9, we must be careful whom we put on our need-to-know list. But think about this: you are the wise, safe, compassionate person for someone else's need-to-know list. You are exactly the person another hurting, confused parent is looking for to walk this journey alongside—not perfectly but as two siblings in Christ who care deeply for their kids.

I remember the first person who showed me she was a kindred spirit in parenting. It was Donna. Her daughter was a challenge to raise. When I shared something small about Katie, she had a similar story about her daughter. She responded with love and compassion toward Katie and me, and I knew I could trust her to journey with me.

As I mentioned at the beginning of the book, once I shared that my kids were making decisions I didn't agree with, I had plenty of other parents to encourage.

Once you get through the tough stuff at the beginning, it's tempting to settle into your new and different (and slightly unexpected!) life. When others come to us at the beginning or middle of their situations, the last thing you want to do is to go back to square one with other parents and help them on their journey. But doing so is part of being the body of Christ. Paul challenges us to be there for each other: "Blessed be the God and Father of our Lord Jesus Christ, the Father of mercies and God of all comfort, who comforts us in all our tribulation, that we may be able to comfort those who are in any trouble, with the comfort with which we ourselves are comforted by God" (2 Corinthians 1:3–4).

Other parents noticed Jan and George being excellent examples of parents loving their son no matter what. Moms were drawn to Jan. Her humility, teachability, wisdom, and love for her son were irresistible to these moms who felt alone, clueless, and helpless. Jan started a group with other moms. She describes it as "a place to be real." What a gift she is to them, and I know they are a gift to her as well. Jan acknowledges it is easy to isolate yourself and not be involved in others' lives.

Of course, reaching out to others is mutually encouraging. Cynthia agrees. "Support systems are wonderful," she says.

Remember James and Lisa's words from chapter 3: "Have other couples you can unload with and pray with together. That kept us afloat." Do you see the transparency in their comment? There is no shame in being real with trusted friends about your situation. Honestly share what your child is up to. Maybe even laugh together over the rhetorical *What are they thinking?* Then encourage and share what works for you.

Keep Turning Your Kids Over to God

Last summer Katie transferred to a different college. She looked online for apartments. She found a couple of places and showed them to us. They looked good, and we agreed to loan her the deposit. She wanted to take care of this task herself, so we didn't go with her to see the apartments. She came home the next day and started the conversation with the tone in her voice that means something we won't like is coming next.

"Um, so, yeah, well, the apartment was five hundred dollars, and if Will shares it with me it will be half of that."

Great. Here we were: back to sharing an apartment with a guy—a friend, but still, she knew how we felt about that.

"We won't loan you the deposit if this is the situation," I reminded her.

"I know. Will put the deposit down so I didn't have to." Katie had her plan before she left to see the apartment. She knew our boundaries, but saving $250 a month was more important than our blessing on her plan.

It's a roller-coaster ride with our kids, isn't it? Just when we think they're on the right track for a little while, they come to us with that tone of voice that warns, *You're not going to agree with this.*

This roller-coaster ride necessitates that we keep turning our kids over to God. It is a continual reminder that we are not in control and we must continue in a walk of faith. Lisa and James find this is an ongoing struggle as they wait for Greg "to come to his senses."

Lisa says, "Do I trust God? I keep turning him over to God."

James shares her same struggle. "It's really stretched, challenged, and threatened my faith. Why has this happened? Where is God in this? I found comfort in this quote, 'As believers we cannot always know why, but *we can always know why we trust God who knows why*, and this makes all the difference.'"[1]

Jan, too, knows the wisdom in celebrating the victories and being prepared for the dips in progress. When we first talked David was moving forward in his life. At that time Jan shared, "I'm thankful, but guarded." Recently I talked with Jan and she says David "took his yearly tumble and is not in a good place right now. . . . He is a loving kid and has potential, but he also has deep issues that return and cycle. So we pray but go on and try to enjoy all the incredible blessings we have through Christ Jesus! God is at work in our kids' lives."

Through years of roller-coaster riding with David, Jan has not become cynical or bitter but accepting of her new normal. She celebrates David's victories but knows he may tumble without warning, and when that happens she'll need to trust God for her son even more.

This takes us back to our discussion on God's love that we started in chapter 9. First John 4:16 reads, "And so we know and rely on the love God has for us. God is love" (NIV). As each of our children goes through ups and downs, we need to rely on the love God has for us and for them. We must trust God with our kids throughout their lives, not just when their lives are going according to our plan for them.

It's a Process

The kids I interviewed all agreed that their journey was a process and that their parents could have done nothing other than *what they did* to bring them back to God. They were on their own journeys. We, the parents, are on journeys as well. Jan reminds us, "Healing is a process. You have to be willing to heal and turn everything over to God." I trust you have made significant progress since you started this book.

If you haven't decided yet, decide now—will you accept this invitation from God to journey with Him? The invitation is presented to you through the circumstances of your child's decisions. God will use these as He can use nothing else to bring to you knowledge of Himself—knowledge that you would not have otherwise. If you cooperate with Him, He will make changes in you to bring you more into the image of His Son. But as Jan said, you must be willing to heal. You will need to let go of expectations for your child and your life. You will need to answer Jesus' question, "Do you want to get well?" (John 5:6 NIV). Jesus asked this question to a man who had been sick for thirty-eight years.

We often want to stay in the comfort of our illness rather than accept the work and risk required to leave that comfort zone for a healthy life. Will you let God heal your bitterness toward your child or toward others who have not been kind? Will you let Him heal your fear of the future? Will you cooperate with Him when He starts the healing process, or will you pick off the scab and let it bleed for all to see?

I know this is hard. You don't have to take big steps or even make a certain amount of progress to make progress. Once in a sermon the speaker shared a visual illustration about making progress toward God when we have nothing to give. He showed a video of his baby (about nine months old) on their hardwood floor. His son wanted to move but could not yet crawl or even bring himself to the crawling position. He would not be discouraged. The little guy flailed his whole body to get it to move across the floor. The speaker gave us another visual illustration. He laid his cell phone on a flat surface and had someone call it. As it rang it vibrated across the flat surface. It looked an awful lot like his baby flailing across the hardwood floor. He challenged us, "If you don't know what to do next or how to get closer to God, can you just flail toward Him?"

When God prompts your heart toward healing, forgiveness, and trust, will you just flail toward Him?

This decision also requires, as Jan wisely stated, turning everything over to God—your child, your pride, your hopes and dreams, your future. Will you repeat the words of Jesus in the Garden of Gethsemane, "Nevertheless not My will, but Yours, be done" (Luke 22:42)? It's scary because we don't know what the will of God will look like in our lives. But we do know it will be for our good and God's glory. How? We rely on God's love for us and for our kids. Nothing is more important than that in our kids' lives. Not other people's perceptions. Not a secure job. Not a house in the suburbs. Not a reputable position in a reputable church. Not our kids living up to the potential God put in them. The most important thing in life is letting God have His way in our kids and cooperating with Him.

This is not an easy journey, in part because we feel as though we journey alone. Remember, our goal is not to be another issue for our kids to deal with. Our goal is, as far as it depends on us, to build a healthy relationship with our kids, because without relationship we have nothing—no influence, no way to help, and no way to show them the way to the Lord. There will be a time for us to speak to our kids about Jesus. But how we live every day with them will be infinitely more powerful and will make the way for our words.

Link arms with your spouse and with other parents. God is with you as you journey with your child and show him or her *I love you no matter what!*

Appendix

The Rest of Their Stories

How the Kids and Their Parents Are Today

I love closure! Just ask my husband. I cannot stop watching a TV show or movie till I see the ending, which often includes watching the credits. While we don't have the ending now or even in this life, I want to share with you where the kids discussed in this book and their parents are in their journeys. Not all are happy or neat, but this is real life.

- Aaron, son of Julie and Marty—Aaron is in his midtwenties and is working in a trade apprenticeship. He got married a few months ago, and he and his wife are doing well. He began paying back the debt to his parents. Once he repented and returned home (by going to and applying counseling and getting a job), Marty and Julie forgave the remainder of the debt. Julie says about the experience, "It really matured him." Aaron, Marty, Julie, and their whole family enjoy a loving, fun, close relationship.

- Allison, daughter of Donna and Bob—Allison is also in her late twenties. Allison and Thomas's marriage is nontraditional in many ways, but it seems to work for them. Allison loves her career. She enjoys a loving, fun relationship with her parents. Thomas prefers the stay on the peripheral. He has turned from the Lord and has become antagonistic toward God. His attitude toward God has become an obstacle to the couple having children. Allison has a detachedness in the areas of marriage where Thomas is harsh and unbending. Donna senses Allison knows she made her choice and must now live with it. Donna and Bob encourage her to make the marriage work. Donna concludes, "The role I have is to pray."

- Andrea, daughter of Cynthia and Frank—Andrea is in her early forties. Her difficult personality keeps her from steadily holding a job, although she is currently employed. Cynthia calls her once a week but doesn't always make contact with Andrea. Cynthia says, "She knows we're there for her. She expresses that a lot. She can come home or call home. There's an open door here."

- Andrew—After five years of immersion in the life and relationships of the church, Andrew is a beautiful example of what it means when Christ makes all things new.

- Brennan, son of Deb—Brennan married his girlfriend, and they have two children. He has his own business.

- David, son of Jan and George—David is in his midtwenties. Jan says, "This fall David took his yearly tumble and is not in a good place right now. He is a loving kid and has potential, but he has deep issues that return and cycle." Jan and George continue in a loving relationship with David while keeping healthy boundaries. "He lived here for two months but managed to get himself back out the door."

- Grace—Grace is in her midthirties. Grace, her husband, and their young children are in the mission field. She is passionate about her work for the Lord. Grace's parents gave her room to process and return to God, and she did. She and her parents began to work on their relationship. Now they are partners in the mission field and love working together.

- Greg, son of Lisa and James—Greg is in his late thirties. He is homeless and jobless. He has turned down all forms of real help and burned everyone who tries to help. James and Lisa stand ready with open arms for his repentance and return. Until then they are holding in place their boundaries. Their hearts continue to ache over Greg's choices.

- Isaac—Isaac is in his late thirties. He has come to the Lord (thanks to his mama's prayers, I'm sure). He is a director in a men's mission for the homeless.

- Jeremy, son of Connie and Robert—Jeremy is still young and trying to find his way. Robert and Connie continue to pursue a relationship with him and give him reasonable boundaries.

- Keith—Keith is in his late thirties. He, his wife, and their three kids are in the mission field overseas. They love their ministry. Keith's parents fully support them, and they enjoy a close, loving relationship.

- Nathan, son of Susan and Gary—Nathan is in his early thirties. He is living back at home and has a good relationship with Susan and Gary. He is back in college. He worked through all the preparation to get into college himself—filling out the application, financial aid, and so on. He is pursuing finding his own apartment. He goes to church with his parents. His biggest challenge is to build new friendships and not fall into the old ones where the temptation is strong. One of his family members shares, "He and God are on the same page with his battle." Isn't that what we want for our kids: to be on the same page with God and working toward the same goal? I want to share one more promising quote from Nathan: "I am now seeing a different world that God has opened for me—the world of feeling good through God. I always loved God through everything. I was just making it hard on myself."

- Katie, daughter of Gene and Brenda (that's me!)—Katie is twenty-five years old. She will graduate college in less than a year and plans on pursuing her master's degree. Our relationship continues to grow. We love her, support her, and encourage her. This past Valentine's Day she made cards for each of the family (that's what artists do!). Gene's card said, "Dad, my hero, I love you!" And my card said, "Mother, I love you!" As I said in the previous pages, Katie still has many views that are different than Gene's and mine. But we are moving forward as a family and she in her life.

Questions for Reflection and Discussion

Chapter 1: Who Are You, and What Have You Done with My Child?

1. Pull out a picture of your child when she was in preschool or kindergarten. Write down a few phrases about what you thought your child's life would look like. Go ahead and grieve what won't be. It's okay. Your life has most likely turned out differently than your parents thought it would too.

2. As you look at your child's picture, list what you loved about your child at that age. Then make another list (even if it's short) of what you love about your child now. Look for things to be thankful for. Often what seems to be a child's weakness is a strength as an adult. I truly believe Katie's determination to live life her way (a.k.a. being a strong-willed child) helped her resist pressures from others to get involved in other temptations.

3. If your child's personality is different from yours or you consistently ram heads with him, pray for and find an adult who has a similar personality. Meet with him and

let him share insights into how and what your child is thinking.

4. Describe your child as a child—personality, characteristics, interests, and so on.
5. Describe your relationship with your child in his childhood.
6. Do you know of an incident or a series of incidents that may have influenced your child to choose a path you don't agree with? Discuss it.
7. What do you think about the implied Christian formula for raising your family that, if followed faithfully, would guarantee your family would mature without any major bumps and bruises?
8. What were your thoughts as you read in Genesis about God's first children behaving so poorly? Were these thoughts new for you? What comfort or encouragement did you take from those passages?
9. Do you ever think you have done something to cause your child to make poor choices? I'm not assigning blame here—just helping you to process your thoughts, maybe for the first time.
10. Be honest and real here—do you long to be the father in Luke 15 with arms open wide for whenever his son returns home?

Chapter 2: What Exactly Are We Talking About?

1. On an index card, list the decisions you are currently in disagreement about with your child. Put each decision under its proper heading (Preference, Foolish, Immoral, or Illegal)

2. On a second index card, write the verse that means the most to you regarding God's love and mercy toward you. Some verses to start with include Deuteronomy 31:8; Psalm 103:8–14, 118:6; Isaiah 40:11 (for you and your child!), 49:15; Romans 8:1; Hebrews 13:5.

3. This week, when you've had it up to here with your child, pray this verse for her.

4. Let's be real with each other. Which of your child's decisions have been a preference—*theirs* was not *yours*? Move them from your foolish and immoral lists, and list them correctly.

5. Have you ever overreacted? Go ahead and give a few of those, writing out the details of those situations.

6. Which of your past or present choices or habits have been foolish, immoral, or illegal? Condense them here.

7. Which of these situations were you grateful to have the mercy of God cover?

8. Have you ever come between your child and the consequences he earned? Share details.

Chapter 3: It Is Not All About You

1. Who will walk with you through this journey? Who has been there—either as the parent or the child? Make contact with those people this week and ask for their support.

2. On an index card, answer Jan's question, "How important is it? In two to three years is it really going to matter?"

3. How much of your motive in dealing with your child is fueled by other people's opinions or your pride?

4. What are you grieving and mourning that will be missing from life as you imagined it?

5. What was once important to you but now not worth losing your relationship with your child over?
6. List your past decisions that your parents did not agree with. Now add those that were dumb, reckless, immoral, or illegal, and ones that you regret.
7. How do you wish your parents would have responded to those decisions?
8. Have you forgiven yourself for your past decisions? Whom else might you need to forgive regarding your past?

Chapter 4: What in the World Am I Doing Wrong?
1. How do you see yourself distancing your kids as the

- Servant Parent—Do you try to woo your child by overcompensating?
- Checked-Out Parent—Have you done all you can— you're done?
- Gotcha! Parent—Do you frequently bringing up your child's issues?
- Passive-Aggressive Parent—Do you neglect to deal with your child's decisions in an honest and direct way? Do you act calm or unaffected when your emotions are churning?
- Scared Parent—Do you feel one wrong move on your part and will cause your child to rebel or bolt so that you'll never see them again?
- Compare and Despair Parent—Do you compare your child's weaknesses against someone else's strengths?

- Controlling Parent—Do you try to gain control over your child by gaining control over the situation?
- You're Ruining My Life Parent—Do you make it clear to your child how she is negatively affecting *your* life?
- My-Way-or-The-Highway Parent—Do you know there are two ways in life—your way and the wrong way?

2. Which parenting style do you see in yourself the most? Why did you pick that one? What is one behavior (word, action, or thought) that made you chose that one?
3. Will you commit to discontinuing this behavior? Brainstorm with a group or your spouse to find a different behavior you can replace the poor behavior with that will show your child you love her no matter what.
4. Time for a light-hearted walk down memory lane. Share with a group or your spouse one issue that you and your parents disagreed on when you were a teen and that you thought you were right about. How did the situation turn out?
5. One of the first things I remember changing in my parenting was to find a list of safe topics I could discuss with Katie so I could rebuild my relationship with her. Sometimes that list was fairly shallow, but it kept us on speaking terms and able to roll over the humps in the relationship road. List two to four topics you can safely discuss with your child.

Chapter 5: What Is Yours and What Is Not

1. Set up a time to apologize to your child. Prayerfully prepare your heart. This conversation will be about you owning your part and expecting nothing in return from your child. Sit humbly at God's feet and let Him show you what you need to confess. Let God share with you His heart for your child so you can keep the main thing the main thing—beginning a healthy relationship with your child—as far as it depends on you (Romans 12:18).

2. Do you speak respectfully to your child and the rest of the family? Double-check your answer with your spouse or a close friend. If you answered *Could do better,* maybe it's time to start a "Disrespect Jar" for the family. Goofy, I know, but sometimes goofy takes the edge off a tense situation. We used to have a jar on the kitchen table. Whenever someone said something negative about someone else or otherwise spoke disrespectfully, he put a quarter in the jar. The money can be used for a fun on a family night.

3. On index cards, list three prayer requests for each of your kids. Use the format below.

   • [Top of the card] God, I know you love my kids more than I do and you want only their best. Help me to see my kids with Your eyes and Your heart.
   • Prayers for (Child 1):
   • Prayers for (Child 2):

   Make at least one of prayer request something you can share with your child at the end of the year. Keep these cards with you and pray for your kids throughout the day.

4. To what extent do you struggle with parental guilt? Have you ever said or thought any of the following statements?

- "It's all my fault."
- "I could have done better as a parent."
- "My kid is messed up and I'm not to blame."

5. List your part in the fray. If you need ideas look back at the list in this chapter.

6. List your child's part in the fray. This is not to dwell on the negative but to help you isolate the real issues so everything isn't an issue.

7. After you read Katie's thoughts on her decision-making process, what are your thoughts about your child and what he's going through? How does Katie's insight help you understand your child better?

8. How do the definitions of *knock*, *ask*, and *seek* change the way you hear Jesus speaking these words to you? How will they change your prayers for your child?

9. Part of our struggle as parents is expecting God to stay within our definitions of good for our kids. Katie recently shared with me that she was thankful for all she has been through because it made her the amazing (my word, not hers) young woman she is today. Looking back, she sees the ugly as being good for her. Share how God used a hard time in your life for your good. Prayerfully place your child in God's hands to accomplish His good His way.

Chapter 6: They Think You Are God (Not Really, but Pretty Close!)

1. From the list of characteristics of God in this chapter, pick one that you have been weak in showing to your child.

   - Compassionate
   - Gracious
   - Slow to anger
   - Loving
   - Patient
   - Available

   Discuss with a group or your spouse one way to show this characteristic of God to your child this week. Write it down.

2. Have you believed any of the lies listed in chapter 6? If yes, which ones? Write down the lies you believe that are keeping you from trusting God and showing God to your child.

3. Every day this week, read the corresponding scripture that demolishes that lie. Prayerfully let God change your mind and accept His truth and healing.

4. Share your answer to Claudia's question: "When did you first realize God's love for you?"

5. If you were raised in church, did your church teach a biblically balanced view of God's love and justice, or did it teeter toward one or the other? If you weren't raised in the church, describe the view of God you pieced together.

6. What impression of God did you receive from your parents?

7. From the list of the characteristics of God, which ones do you show to your child?

Chapter 7: Oh, So That's How to Be a Cool Parent

1. Discuss with your spouse your nonnegotiables. Now list them. Is there anything that is news to your kids? During a time of non-conflict, matter-of-factly and without emotion inform your kids of the "change in policy." No discussion needs to follow.

2. Think of one way, no matter how small, you can be involved in your child's life this week. I've listed a few ideas. Don't let seven days pass before you do that one thing.

   - Take your child on a coffee/lunch/breakfast date.
   - Mail or deliver to your child a care package. Include items such as coffee, cookies, cute tissues, notepads, gift cards, and a note of encouragement from you.
   - Invite your child to dinner and a movie.
   - Call for no reason.
   - Let technology work for you—text, Facebook message, or e-mail a word of encouragement, fun picture, or something you found on the Internet worthy of sharing.

3. What facet of who you are might be helpful in connecting with your child? In what way could you use that part of your personality to connect with your child in the next month or so?

4. This week, sit down with your spouse and determine your money policy. If it will change the status quo, include it in the nonnegotiable briefing in #1.

5. Own up to one area where your child pushes your button every time. Why? In light of the importance of building a healthy relationship with your child, how will you handle this situation next time?

6. While we're on the subject, what topic or issue in your child's life do you comment about frequently—in other words, which of your child's buttons do you push? Make a commitment with your spouse, group, or friend that you will keep your mouth shut the next time you're tempted to speak an unnecessary, unedifying comment to your child.

7. If I interviewed your child, would he respond like Nathan that, even when he was giving his parents a hard time, he knew they genuinely cared about him and listened to what he said? If not, what is between you and your child?

8. Think of a relationship in which you feel safe to be yourself. What about the other person makes you feel this way? How could you offer this same gift to your child?

9. How hard is it for you to let your child take his consequences? Why? Do you see the need for your child to deal with his consequences? Commit to your spouse or friend that you will not interfere next time, and give that person permission to hold you accountable. If you are in the habit of intervening for your child, calmly confess your sin in doing this, ask his forgiveness, and then tell him you won't be doing so in the future.

Chapter 8: The Learning Curve

1. Are you a backstage parent or a parent who has taken her seat midway in the auditorium? If you have been a backstage parent, write an apology to your child for being intrusive in her life. (Be ready to catch her if she faints when she reads it.) Then tell her you are taking your seat in the auditorium and let her how much you look forward to cheering her on. If you are already have a seat in the auditorium, offer your child a word of encouragement or give her a gift certificate for a special time with you.

2. If your child is living in the distant country, are you sending the servant to him with money to live on? Are you enabling your child to live comfortably in his distant country? If you are, write down one thing you can do now to let him feel the consequences of his poor choices. Date your commitment and have a trusted friend, another couple, your counselor, or someone witness it.

3. I love visual aids! To help you remember to pursue your life, thus "containing the crisis" of your child, find a coffee can (it doesn't have to be metal), fill it with dirt, and plant a flower or other small plant. Water this precious plant and care for it. Let it serve as a reminder that even though you love and care about your child, his life is only a part of yours, and your life continues to go on.

4. How hard is it for you to hold expectations of your child loosely while he's in process? If you're already keeping your expectations low, share an example.

5. Let's practice backing off without cutting off. Ask a friend to pretend to be your child and present a

situation your child might come to you with. Give
your "child" biblical, no-strings-or-emotions-attached
advice.

6. Do you understand that this process is about you as well
   as your child? What is God speaking to you about that
   He wants to change? Write it down, and add a line or
   two to God promising that you will cooperate with how
   He is working in you.

7. What is your child's issue? Do you need to learn more
   about it so you can help him and yourself better? See
   the resources in the back of the book. Find help.

8. How are your child's decisions affecting your marriage?
   Look over the suggestions in the chapter and decide
   which one might help you and your spouse. If nothing
   looks like a good fit, talk to a trusted couple or friend
   for suggestions on whom to see for help.

Chapter 9: Everybody Is Talking

1. Do you struggle to absorb the reality of God's
   unconditional love for you? It's okay. It's a process. For
   the next week, every morning before you get out of bed,
   meditate on Zephaniah 3:17: "God . . . will quiet you with
   his love . . . rejoice over you with singing." With whom will
   you share this love, and how will you do it?

2. Let's follow Jan's advice and come up with a short
   response to those who pry or offer unsolicited advice.
   Jan's response was, "I'm so thankful God's at work in his
   life." My grandpa had a couple of clever responses to nosy
   questions. One was, "Now why would you want to know a
   thing like that?" I know that's a silly response for a serious

subject, but maybe that's your style. Write a few responses on an index card so you'll be ready ahead of time.

3. If you're doing this book in a group, go to the Practical Application Page and work on number two together. Have a little fun with it, but come up with a short, gracious sentence.

4. How do you feel about creating a need-to-know list of people who care about and will help you and your child? Who is on your need-to-know list? Other parents? Professionals? Young adults who experienced your kid's journey? Who do you need to add? Pray for guidance, and then make the contact.

5. If your particular church is not being helpful in your specific situation, prayerfully consider whether a different church would help your family. Remember, your local church is a small part of the body of Christ. Other churches are part of the same body, and we can worship there too.

6. How did your attitude change toward kids in your church who weren't "following the rules" after one of your own kids didn't follow the rules?

7. Discuss the difference between the definitions of *judge*—(1) to try, condemn, or punish, and (2) to investigate, determine, or question. What is the difference in the heart attitude between the two? Which is your tendency?

8. How do you (or do you) rely on God's love each day? What else do you rely on? In our culture there are so many options—our jobs, our money, our educations, our technological "other halves," our good health, our

spouses, our roles in the church, and so on. If you had none of the above, then would you rely on God's love?

9. What would it take for you to know and feel accepted and cherished by God? To have His peace even though every issue is not settled in your life? To know and accept that the blood of Christ has cleansed you from your past and you have no more shame? Recall Romans 8:1: "There is therefore now no condemnation to those who are in Christ Jesus, who do not walk according to the flesh, but according to the Spirit." Will you rely on God's love and share it with others?

10. Did you go through a period of denial that your child could be involved in anything sketchy? How did you discover something was up? If appropriate, will you thank those involved in sharing your child's behavior with you?

Chapter 10: Happy Ending

1. Pull out pictures (or videos) of you and your kids having fun and making memories when they were young. Place a couple of these in your Bible or journal and use them as encouragement as you pray. If possible, ask your children to tell you some of their cherished memories of what you did with them. Write the memories on an index card and place it with the picture.

2. If you haven't done so already, ask God for another parent to pray with you (even over the phone) for your child. Make the contact and set a time.

3. If you have decided to do what it takes to be part of
   your child's life, where are you in your journey? Are you
   letting God heal you? Here's a plan to cooperate with
   God's healing in you.

   • When you sense God changing your thoughts
     about a person or situation, instead of going back
     to bitterness, choose forgiveness. Think about the
     flailing baby on the hardwood floor, or set your cell
     phone to vibrate and have someone call it. Just flail
     towards God, even if you can't take a big step.
   • When you feel fear coming on, recognize it and
     don't let it take control of your thoughts. Instead,
     give your fear to God and rely on His love. Try this:
     Say, "This is fear. It ignores God in my life. God is
     love, and I rely on God's love for me and my child."
     When a thought comes to mind that tempts you to
     revisit past pain or have a pity party (equivalent to
     picking off a scab), stop your thoughts and repeat
     the process above, speaking the truth of God's
     involvement in your life. I love Joshua 1:5 (NASB): "I
     will be with you; I will not fail you or forsake you."
     Then move on with your day.

4. Are in you in or out? Will you do what it takes to be part
   of your child's life? Make your commitment out loud to
   your group or your spouse.
5. Okay, by now we all know that none of us are
   perfect parents, and we probably have a long list of
   "should've's." What is one way you will start to build

your relationship with your child this week? Maybe start with a card saying how sorry you are for the past and how much you love them.

6. Is your family enjoying life or living with a storm cloud overhead? I know it's easy to let that cloud park over your house. I remember our first vacation without Katie. We missed her, and she missed us. She could have come, but she didn't want to commit to a whole week with us. But we had fun—the least of which was that Kelsey and Kerry discovered cable TV! Make plans to do one fun thing (dinner, movie, vacation) as a family or a couple. If your prodigal wants to come and behave herself, great. If not, life goes on.

7. How will you be there for other parents? As you reach out to others, think about what you needed at the beginning of your experience: acceptance, someone who will listen, and one practical thing to do next.

8. How difficult is it to continually trust God with your child? Do you rely on God's love for you and your child? You and God have this!

With God you can make a difference in your child's life. My prayer for you is that you draw near to God, letting Him comfort you, guide you, and change you. I pray your child will come to the Lord. I pray for healthy, loving, God-glorifying relationships for you and your family.

Notes

Chapter 1: Who Are You, and What Have You Done with My Child?

1. "Maturation of the Prefrontal Cortex," US Department of Health and Human Services, Office of Population Affairs, last modified October 2012, http://hhs.gov/opa/familylife/tech_assistance/etraining/adolescent_brain/Development/prefrontal_cortex/index.html.
2. Josh McDowell, *The Last Christian Generation* (Holiday, FL: Green Key Books, 2006), 13.
3. George Barna, *Real Teens* (Ventura, CA: Regal Books, 2001), 136.
4. James Strong, *Strong's Exhaustive Concordance of the Bible* (Iowa Falls, IA: AMG Publishers, 1986), New Testament 60 and 67.
5. Ibid., New Testament 31.

Chapter 2: What Exactly Are We Talking About?

1. Brenda Garrison, *Queen Mom: A Royal Plan for Restoring Order in Your Home* (Cincinnati: Standard Publishing, 2007).
2. James Strong, *Strong's Exhaustive Concordance of the Bible* (Iowa Falls, IA: AMG Publishers, 1986), Old Testament 74.
3. Ibid., New Testament 65.
4. Ibid., Old Testament 74.
5. http://dictionary.reference.com/browse/folly.
6. http://www.cdc.gov/features/heartmonth/.
7. Ibid.
8. Strong, *Concordance*, New Testament 57.

Chapter 3: It Is Not All About You

1. Arlene Eisenberg, Sandee Hathaway, and Heidi Murkoff, *What to Expect When You're Expecting* (New York: Workman Publishing, 1984).

Chapter 5: What Is Yours and What Is Not

1. Oswald Chambers, *My Utmost for His Highest* (Urichsville, OH: Barbour Publishing Inc., 1963), 49.
2. Wayne Grudem, *Systematic Theology* (Grand Rapids: Zondervan, 1994), 333.
3. Ibid.
4. James Strong, *Strong's Exhaustive Concordance of the Bible* (Iowa Falls, IA: AMG Publishers, 1986), New Testament 84.
5. Ibid., New Testament 5 and 51.

Chapter 6: They Think You Are God (Not Really, but Pretty Close!)

1. Wayne Grudem, *Systematic Theology* (Grand Rapids: Zondervan, 1994), 204.
2. Tim Kimmel, *Grace-Based Parenting* (Nashville: Thomas Nelson, 2004), 16.
3. James Strong, *Strong's Exhaustive Concordance of the Bible* (Iowa Falls, IA: AMG Publishers, 1986), Old Testament 53.
4. Charles Caldwell Ryrie, Th.D., Ph.D., *Ryrie Study Bible* (Chicago: Moody Publishers, 1976, 1978), 1337.
5. Grudem, *Systematic Theology*, 201.
6. Oswald Chambers, *My Utmost for His Highest* (Urichsville, OH: Barbour Publishing Inc., 1963), 7.

Chapter 8: The Learning Curve

1. Teen Challenge is an organization that provides youth, adults, and families with an effective and comprehensive Christian solution to drug and alcohol problems. For more information, see http://teenchallengeusa.com/program.

Chapter 9: Everbody Is Talking

1. James Strong, *Strong's Exhaustive Concordance of the Bible* (Iowa Falls, IA: AMG Publishers, 1986), New Testament 57.
2. Ibid., New Testament 11.

Chapter 10: Happy Ending

1. Os Guinness, *In Two Minds: The Dilemma of Doubt and How to Resolve It* (Downers Grove, IL: InterVarsity Press, 1976), 255.

Resources

Al-Anon—"Strength and Hope for Families and Friends of Problem Drinkers." Visit http://www.al-anon.alateen.org.

Boundaries: When to Say Yes, When to Say No to Take Control of Your Life by Dr. Henry Cloud and Dr. John Townsend.

Boundaries with Teens by Dr. John Townsend.

Boundaries with Kids: How Healthy Choices Grow Healthy Children by Lisa Guest, Dr. Henry Cloud, and Dr. John Townsend.

The Five Love Languages of Children by Dr. Gary Chapman and Dr. Ross Campbell.

The Five Love Languages of Teens New Edition: The Secret to Loving Teens Effectively by Dr. Gary Chapman.

Focus on the Family—Radio program and website with helpful information on all issues families face. Visit http://www.focusonthefamily.com/, or contact them directly for help at http://family.custhelp.com/app/home.

Teen Challenge—Mission Statement: "To provide youth, adults and families with an effective and comprehensive Christian faith-based solution to life-controlling drug and alcohol problems in order to become productive members of society. By applying biblical principles, Teen Challenge endeavors to help people become mentally-sound, emotionally-balanced, socially-adjusted, physically-well, and spiritually-alive." Visit http://teenchallengeusa.com/program.

About the Authors

Brenda Garrison is an enthusiastic and authentic speaker and author. She ministers to women in all stages of life but especially to moms—encouraging them by keeping it real and based on God's Word. Brenda speaks at retreats, workshops, professional groups, and government agencies that work with families. She has appeared on *FamilyLife Today*, Moody Radio, and *The Harvest Show*, as well as other media outlets. Brenda and her husband, Gene, have three daughters and live in Illinois.

Katie Garrison is a college student and talented artist. Her artwork is currently displayed prominently throughout her parents' home, but hopefully someday her art will be enjoyed by countless others. Katie will graduate soon with a bachelor's degree in fine arts, with a concentration in 3D studio, after which she plans to pursue a master's degree in fine arts.

CPSIA information can be obtained at www.ICGtesting.com
Printed in the USA
LVOW130706210812

295225LV00005B/1/P